The Habsburg's Venetian War of 1487

... or the War of Rovereto

Florian Messner / Hagen Seehase

Translation by Richard Sanders

"Whichever of the two should cry "Catherina,"
he should have lost the battle and the money"

*(From the Pappenheim Chronicle about the duel
between Johann von Waldburg-Sonnenberg and Antonio Maria da Sanseverino)*

Authors:	Florian Messner & Hagen Seehase
Translator:	Richard Sanders
Illustrations:	Sascha Lunyakov
Map:	Bernhard Glänzer
Publisher:	Zeughaus Verlag GmbH
	Knesebeckstr. 88
	10623 Berlin, Germany
	Telephone: +49 (0)30/315 700 30
	Email: info@zeughausverlag.de
	Website: www.zeughausverlag.de

All rights reserved.
Reproduction, translation and photographic reproduction, including extracts are forbidden. Storage and distribution including transfer onto electronic media like CD-ROM etc. as well as storage on electronic media like the Internet etc. are not permissible without the express written permission of the publisher and are punishable.
Bibliographic information from the Deutschen Bibliothek: The Deutsche Bibliothek lists this publication in the German National Bibliography; detailed bibliographic information is available at http://dnb.ddb.de

Printed in European Union
Originally published in German as *"Der Venezianerkrieg"*
in the Heere & Waffen series numbers 35
(Berlin: Zeughaus Verlag, 2020)

© 2020 Zeughaus Verlag GmbH, Berlin, Germany
ISBN: 978-3-96360-027-2

The cover illustration shows two soldiers with armor well suited for rapid attack, for example to take a town in a surprise attack.

ACKNOWLEDGEMENTS

Our thanks to Stefan Müller and the whole team from Zeughaus-Verlag who made this book possible. Additionally, we want to thank Jens Peter Kleinau whose description of the individual combat between Johann von Waldburg-Sonnenberg and Antonio Maria da Sanseverino (available in the noteworthy blog talhoffer.wordpress.com) was one of the most important inspirations for this book. In addition, we thank him for the foreword to this book. Photos were provided by Anja and Michael Hiebinger from the Veldenzer Aufgebot (Veldenz Levy reenactment group), Michel Sicher from the Condottieri Mauriziani reenactment group, along with Arma Georgii and Fred Wutz. Richard J. Kyte and Christopher Retsch were also of assistance with illustrations.

We also owe thanks to the Italian reenactment group Città del Griffo for the photos they contributed.

Special thanks to Michael Sicher for arranging important contacts.

We especially thank Wolfgang Braun for the wonderful reconstruction illustrations.

For the pictures of swords, we thank Stefan Roth, who also made these weapons himself.

We would like to thank Bernhard Glänzer and Sasha Lunyakov for their illustrations.

Special thanks to Moritz Seeburger, who gave important advice.

Last but not least, we would like to thank Richard Sanders and his daughter-in-law, Raluca Sanders, for the translation. This translation is thanks to their diligence, his understanding of military history, and her linguistic skills and talent for quickly familiarizing herself with new topics.

Contents

Chronology	8
Foreword	9
Author's Preliminary Note	9
The Venetian Republic and Italy in the 15th Century	10
Duke Sigismund "The Rich in Coin" (*"der Münzreiche"*)	18
The *Guerra Retica* and its Causes	31
The Outbreak of Hostilities	35
Rovereto	41
The Duel	46
Gaudenz von Matsch Withdraws	49
The Battle of Calliano	53
The Aftermath	58
Warfare at the Time of the Rovereto War	62
The Tirolian Forces	62
The Venetian Forces	82
The Battle in the Enne Mountains	93
List of the Persons Involved in the Conduct of the Duel	95
Bibliography	96

CHRONOLOGY

26 October 1427: Birth of the later Archduke Sigismund of Tirol

1443–1446: Sigismund is under his uncle's guardianship

9 April 1446: Sigismund's release from the guardianship

28 April 1446: Sigismund's entry as the ruler in Tirol

Starting 1458: Sigismund's conflicts with the Swiss Confederation

1460: Height of the conflict between Duke Sigismund and Bishop Nikolaus Cusanus

5 September 1469: Treaty of St. Omer, pledging of the greater part of the Austrian Outlands to Duke Charles the Bold as collateral

30 March 1474: Perpetual Accord (*Ewige Richtung*), alliance between Sigismund and the Swiss

1474–1477: Burgundian Wars

1477: Sigismund's elevation to Archduke

1486: Negotiations between Tirol and Venice by the Prince Bishop of Trento, Johannes Hinderbach

Beginning of 1487: So-called "Poisoning Affair" at the Innsbruck court

March 1487: Confiscation of Venetian goods by Archduke Sigismund

23 April 1487: Arrest of Venetian merchants in Tirol

9 May 1487: Swiss Confederation's refusal to provide assistance to Sigismund

May 1487: Assembling of a Tirolian army; naming of Count Gaudenz von Matsch as the commander in chief

30 May 1487: Capture of the town of Rovereto by Tirolian forces

June 1487: Count Roberto da Sanseverino d´Aragona named as the new Venetian commander in chief

11 June 1487: Fall of the Rovereto Castle to the Tirolians

12 June 1487: Duel between Antonio Maria da Sanseverino and Johann von Waldburg-Sonnenberg

13 June 1487: Arrival at the Tirolians of reinforcements from the Swiss *Orte*.

3 July 1487: Battle at Ravazzone, capture of Antonio Maria da Sanseverino by the Tirolians

July 1487: Sigismund's secret treaty with Duke Albrecht of Bavaria-Munich for financing of a campaign against Venice; Graudenz's unexpected withdrawal from Matsch

25 July 1487: Recapture of Rovereto by the Venetians, siege of Castel Pietra by the Venetians

End of July 1487: Friedrich Kappler becomes commandant of the city of Trento

Beginning of August 1487: Tirol's military successes in the *Giudicarie*; concentration of the Tirolian units from the *Giudicarie* and from Lake Garda to Trient/Trento

10 August 1487: Battle of Calliano, Tirol's victory under Kappler, death of Roberto da Sanseverino

16 August 1487: Dismissal of the "Bad Counselors" by Archduke Sigismund

October 1487: Negotiations between Tirol and Venice

13 November 1487: Treaty concluded between Tirol and Venice

November 1487: New court and laws in Tirol

1490: Abdication of the Archduke Sigismund as Tirol's regent

4 March 1496: Archduke Sigismund's death in Innsbruck

FOREWORD

The reconstruction of the "historical combat," i.e., the combat with medieval weapons, requires constant, intensive research as well as being done in a practical and historical context. It is not enough to just know how to and to practice swinging a sword. Without that necessary background, any practice is worthless because historical personal combat, as in a duel, is anchored is anchored deep in history, because personal combat was not the same as fighting and the rules for fighting could vary significantly. For example, a knightly duel could be governed by discretionary rules. If a combatant wanted to spare his warhorse, then the horses would be excluded from the striking zone. In another duel, the number of blows could be limited. In the fencing instructor's school and the artisans' associations blows to the hands and legs and body-slamming were forbidden. In the knightly tournaments, the opponents, separated by barriers, smashed away their swords on their steel armor. The variety of the combats and competitions is impressive. But unfortunately we seldom get more information about a combat than its outcome. The historical sources that describe an engagement in detail are extremely rare and valuable.

The knightly duel between Johann von Waldburg-Sonnenberg and Antonio Maria da Sanseverino is a special jewel in historic records that is confirmed by several sources. It rightly takes a central part of this work. The duel between these two noblemen in the setting of the campaign of 1487 was especially dramatic. Indeed, as the historic art of combat cannot be seen without the context of history, this thrilling duel would be a meaningless anecdote without its being viewed in history.

In this book, the authors, Florian Messner and Hagen Seehase, present the historic context skillfully. The story offers everything that today's pay television series create with so much effort: prominent characters fighting for power and money, with intrigues, treachery and death, marriages without love – therefore based on lust for power – and dark politics with huge battle scenes. Amidst this there are heroic duels. The actual history is often more exciting and dramatic than the invented.

Jens Peter Kleinau, 2019

AUTHORS' PRELIMINARY NOTE

The events presented in this book took place partially in German-speaking, but also in part in Italian- or Ladin-speaking regions.

The way people's and place names are presented is oriented on what culture they belonged to at the time of the events. In order to avoid misunderstanding and to facilitate later access to descriptions – when necessary – both versions appear, for example, like "Görz" and (Italian) "Gorizia".

For the names of large towns, cities and regions, the English names have been used, e.g., "Venice" and not "Venezia."[1]

Names of rulers, etc. are retained in their native language, so "Charles VII" and not "Karl VII."[2] For the Popes' names of the familiar English names have been used.

---

[1] In the original German edition of this book, German names were used for large towns, cities and regions.

[2] In the original version, German names were used for the Popes.

THE VENETIAN REPUBLIC AND ITALY IN THE 15th CENTURY

In the 15th century, Italy was a geographic and cultural concept – but not a political one. Italy was culturally much more homogenous than many European kingdoms of that time. The Western Roman Empire had long since ceased to exist, but the religion and legal system continued from the late phase of the Empire. The Italian language, derived from Latin, had been spoken since the 7th century. The Italian used by the poets of the Sicilian School since the 12th century is still understood today. Common culture and customs united the inhabitants of the Italian peninsula. However, political unification was a long way off. It consisted of many independent principalities. Sardinia (which had the status of a kingdom since 1239) was a viceroyship possessed by Aragon. The Kingdom Sicily was also an Aragon possession. Mainland Sicily, also a kingdom,[3] was fought over frequently, but in the 15th century was normally ruled by kings from the Aragon house. In central Italy lay the Papal State ruled by the Pope as the worldly ruler. Then there were also the Republics of Florence, Genoa, Venice, Lucca, Siena and San Marino. Among the smaller principalities were Piombino and Monaco, while Saluzzo had the status of a margraveship. Modena, Mantua, Massa, Ferrara, Urbino and Carrara had the status of duchies.[4] Milan was, except from the short intermediate phase when it was the "Ambrosian Republic", also a duchy.

It is noteworthy that Venetian possessions outside Italy were significantly larger than within the land. Venetian territories were located not only on the Adriatic coasts but also everywhere in the eastern Mediterranean. Before the 1453 fall of Constantinople, there was even a Venetian base in the Crimea. Venetian features with regard to politics and society in the 15th century have to be understood in the context of Venetian history.

When in the 5th century AD the hordes from the migrations broke into the Italian peninsula, many of the inhabitants of the upper Adria fled to the offshore islands in the Venetian Lagoon. The threat by the Huns under their legendary King Atilla especially drove thousands of refugees to the safe islands.

As part of the Exarchate of Ravenna,[5] Venice was officially under Byzantine rule in the 6th century. Due to the increasing threat posed by the Lombards and other tribes, more and more people moved to the islands in the lagoon. As a result, Venice increased in importance, while the lands on the coast declined economically. According to legend, recounted by Paoluccio Anafesto from Eraclea, in the year 697 twelve leading families[6] of the city rose up, the most noble among them became the first doge.[7] He was followed by 119 more doges, until the Venetian Republic ended in 1797 in the turmoil of the Napoleonic Wars.

Like so many legends from the early middle ages, it is possible the first doge was an invention from a later time. Therefore, Orso Ipato, who ruled from 726 to 737 as the head of the republic and who was named by the people's assembly, is considered to have been the first doge. The doge had both military and judicial authority and with that, he was the absolute ruler of the Republic for life.

Along with the power, there also came the temptation to create a family dynasty as was common in the Middle Ages in the Italian peninsula's other city states. Venice's families wanted to prevent that - the doge was to be the "primus inter pares" (first among equals) and in no way rule in an authoritarian manner. Starting with the 12th century, a complex selection process developed, which took place after the death of a doge and was overseen by a 40-man commission. Besides, starting in the mid-12th century, the "Great Council"[8] could put the doge aside. This council controlled not only the republic but also elected the doges.[9]

In order to ensure the effective governance, in the 15th century the "Minor Council *Consiglio Minore*" developed, better known as "Signoria". It complemented the doge's power and, if needed, could depose him. Among other things, every year the Council named over 400 vari-

---

3   This territory is sometimes called the "Kingdom of Naples". Until 1320, together with the island of Sicily it formed a kingdom.

4   Compare Paoletti, Ciro, *A Military History of Italy* (Westport und London: Praeger Security International, 2008), p. 4.

5   The Exarchate of Ravenna was a Byzantine administrative district in northeast Italy and included the western Adriatic coast from Ravenna to Perugia. It was founded around 584 and was supposed to protect the Eastern Roman rule from the Lombards. Gradually all the parts of the Exarchate were lost until the Lombard King Aistulf conquered Ravenna in 751.

6   The numerous noble families were canonized starting in 1350 so that there was a group of 24 (or 25) "*case vecchie*" (old noble houses), who rose in power and influence over the newer nobles ("*case nuove*"). These old families were divided into two groups, the "*duodecim nobiliorum proles Venetiarum*" and the "*que in nobilitate secuntur stirpes XII superius memoratas*". These families provided the doges and attempted again and again to found dynasties. The best-known families were the Bado, Barossi, Dandolo or Tiepolo

7   The term "*doge*" comes from the Italian and is a modification of the Latin "*dux*", which essentially means a chief. In the late antiquity, the most senior military commander in the border provinces was designated as a "*dux*." The office of the doge existed in Genoa among other places but the one in Venice was by far the most powerful and enduring. As a sign of his power, starting in the 14th century the Doge of Venice wore the typical headwear of the "*corno ducale*", a Phrygian cap with a horn on a diadem crown around it.

8   This "*Maggior Consiglio*" was composed of the city's leading families that initially changed but starting in 1297 ("Serrata") was firmly established. In the Great Council were seated all male representatives of the old noble houses so that at the beginning of the 16th century it had more than 2,000 members.

9   The Republic was by modern standards in no way a democracy, but rather an oligarchy in which the most powerful families determined the particular ruler.

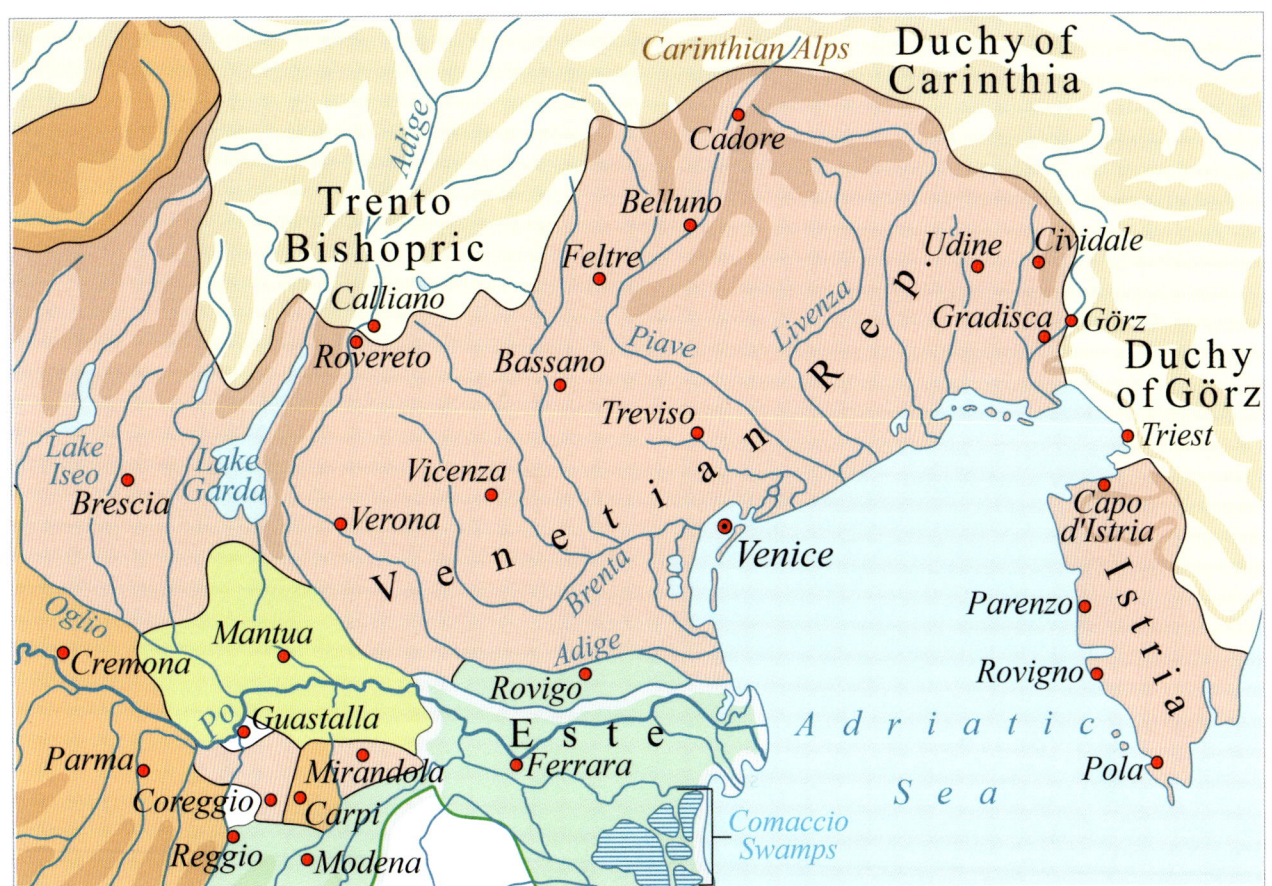

Venice's Italian possessions ca. 1480.
Map: Bernhard Glänzer

ous officials so that a highly complex power apparatus developed, and that continued to function for several hundred years.[10]

With the doge at its head, Venice could keep the advancing armies of the migrating tribes at a distance. The conquest of the Exarchate of Ravenna by the Lombards in 751 even strengthened Venice in the long term. Then based on its advantageous location it soon became the center of maritime trade in the Adriatic. The official title of the city on the Lagoon was *"Serenissima Repubblica di San Marco"* - "The Most Serene Republic of Saint Mark".[11]

Today one associates the name Venice above all with the island in the world-famous lagoon. In the course of the Middle Ages and early modern times the Serenissima was disproportionately expansive. Thanks to its brilliant traders in the focal point between the Orient and the Occident, an economic metropolis developed that invested its millions in trade, in mercenary armies and fleets in order to constantly expand its lands. The preliminary high point of this striving for power was the Fourth Crusade, when in 1204 the Venetians succeeded in diverting the Crusader army that was actually supposed to liberate Egypt to go to Constantinople.[12] The Latin Empire was erected on the ruins of the city that was more than obligated to Venice. Thus the Serenissima was able to occupy extensive parts of the Peloponnesus and the surrounding islands, among others Crete, Euböe (Italian: *Negroponte*) and Cyprus.[13]

The terms *"Dogado"* (the actual lagoon with the coastal strip), *"Domini di Terra Ferma"* (the possessions on the mainland, above all in northern Italy) and *"Stato di Mar"* (the possessions in the eastern Mediterranean region) arose for the new sphere of control.

---

10 Along with these institutions there were a series of additional groups, which in part had overlapping functions, among them the Senate, the College of Wise Men (*"Collegio dei Savi"*), the Council of Forty (*"Quarantia"*) and the Council of Ten (*"Consiglio dei Dieci"*).

11 Saint Markus has been the city's patron saint since 828 when Venetian merchants stole the saint's reliquary from Alexandria and buried it in the current Cathedral of St. Mark. For that reason, Venice to this day has the winged lion of St. Mark in its coat of arms.

12 During the sack of the city, the Venetians looted the four world-famous, bronze statues of horses (the *Quadriga*) that today decorate the Cathedral of St. Mark. These are the only existing Quadriga from ancient Rome that probably date back to the 3rd-4th century AD.

13 Venetian rule over the Aegean lasted into the 16th century when the Ottoman Empire gradually conquered the islands.

On the Italian Peninsula, Venice found itself in constant conflict with the bordering city states. The trading metropolises and maritime republics of Genoa and Pisa especially opposed the Serenissima on land and at sea. In the Chioggia War (1378-1381) Venice was finally, after a bitter struggle, able to drive the Genoese from the Adriatic ending their competition in the eastern Mediterranean region.

Thereupon, the Doge Michele Steno (1400-1413) forced the aggressive expansion on the Italian mainland, the Terra Ferma. After Verona had already been incorporated, after the death of Milan's ruler Gian Galeazzo Visconti in 1402, almost all of Veneto, Friuli and also parts of Dalmatia came under Venice's rule. This policy displeased Emperor Sigismund (1368-1437) because the regions were actually part of the Holy Roman Empire. Between 1411 and 1420 there were wars, two of which were very intensive, from which Venice emerged as the victor and expanded its borders to the Counties of Tirol and Gorizia (German: Görz) in the north.

Emperor Sigismund had to submit to ignomiy and in 1437 granted the Terra Ferma and Dalmatia to the Doge Marco Dandolo as imperial fiefs. To do this, Doge Marco made a special trip to the Emperor's court in Prague in order to publicly secure the political victory. The Dogato, i.e., the island in the Lagoon, explicitly was excluded because it still officially belonged to the Eastern Roman Empire.

Encouraged by these successes, the Doges hired the most famous *Condottieri* of their time. These mercenary leaders commanded their own units that put themselves at the disposal of a master for a certain duration.

For example, Erasmo di Narni, called "Gattamelata",[14] and Francesco Bussone,[15] called "Carmagnola," went into the service of the Doge and spread war across the northern Italian cities. The expansion's main target was above all the disintegrating Duchy of Milan. The Doge Francesco Foscari (1427–1453) had his troops drive deep into Lombardy, the important fortress cities of Brescia and Bergamo fell, and in 1433 Venice stood on the banks of the River Adda, barely 30 kilometers from Milan.

In the following years, Milan succeeded in striking back and in 1438 in besieging Brescia. Gattamelata was able to break out with his force of nearly 3,000 man and get through to the north and reach Venetian territory by way of a circuitous route.[16]

But Brescia continued to put up resistance to Milan, and so the Serenissima made plans to relieve the city. All of the road connections were, however, occupied by the enemy plus Lake Garda formed a natural barrier. Therefore, the Venetians decided on one of military history's most daring endeavors: capturing Lake Garda with ships from the Adriatic.

However, the undertaking to which they committed themselves faced a huge challenge because the Milanese controlled the lake's north, south and west parts and thus also the of the inlets. Gattamelata therefore conceived a bold plan that was implemented immediately. A Venetian fleet was brought up the Adige River and then moved about 20 kilometers by land to Lake Garda. After a remarkable victory on Lake Garda in 1440 the Venetians could finally succeed in the North. In a final desperate alliance with Florence, Bologna and Cremona, the Milanese ruler Filippo Maria Visconti (1392–1447) was still able to fend off the Venetians' attacks. Yet at the battle of Castelmaggiore, Venice was able to grasp victory and drive the Milanese from Visconti. The wars against Milan ended with the 1454 Treaty of Lodi in which Venice was conceded all of its conquests east of the Adda.

For now, the Serenissima had cemented its predominance in Northern Italy. It stretched in the south to past Ferrara, in the west to the Adriatic and in the north and east to the domains of the Habsburgs: Krain (Carniola), Görz (Gorizia) and Tirol.

During the reign of the 72nd doge, Giovanni Moncenigo, the 16-year war with the Turks ended in 1479, but Venice had to accept bitter losses of territories in the Eastern Mediterranean. Furthermore, there were sporadic outbreaks of the plague. Because of conflicts with Florence and Ferrara, Venice was anathematized. Giovanni Moncenigo died on 4 November 1485 and soon thereafter his successor, Marco Barbarigo, passed away on 14 August 1486. The rumor circulated that he had been murdered.[17]

His brother, Agostino Barbarigo, became the 74th doge. He was noted for his military experience, but also for his tendency to nepotism and self-importance and he was not uncontroversial in Venice.

---

14   1370-1443. His nickname essentially meant "honey-colored cat" and was supposed to refer to his shrewdness, and also ability to get out of tough situation victoriously. Gattamelata was one of Italy's most successful *Condottieri*, fought for the Pope, Florence and finally for Venice where he rose to captain general. The high point of his military career was in 1439 capture of Verona from the Visconti. As the ruler of Padua, he was also a great patron of the arts so that the famous Renaissance artist Donatello produced a life-size bronze equestrian statue of Gattamelata – the first since ancient Rome.

15   1380–1432. Francesco came from the family of counts from Carmagnola, therefore the nickname. Next to Gattamelata he was certainly the best-known Venetian Condottiere. He began his career in Milan's service, even married a Visconti and in 1425 finally changed sides to Venice. In the victorious battle of Maclodio against Milan (1427 Carmagnola devised enormous crossbows, which he mounted on carts. After a defeat by Milan, the Council of Ten accused him of treason and had him publicly beheaded. His confession was, however, obtained under torture and today it is thought that Carmagnola was misused as an escape goat.

16   Gattamelata was named Venice's military Commander in Chief for this tactical masterstroke.

17   But this conjecture is most probably inaccurate. Compare Bertolizio, Giorgio, *Dogi; Nullità al potere* (Rome: Lit Edizioni, 2013), p. 233.

This group of foot soldiers is primarily equipped with polearms that are also called "Italian halberds".
Photo: Città del Grifo

Transporting the Venetian ships overland to Lake Garda
Engraving by Giuseppe Lorenzo Gatteri from the year 1852.

Portrait of the Doge Agostino Barbarigo
Author's archives

Venetian Official ▶
Photo: Condottieri Mauriziani

Halberds and bills
("*Roßschindern*" - "horse flayers") were still contemporary weapons, but the polearm's twilight had begun.
Photo: Città del Grifo

For the militiamen of the northern Italian cities, like for the numerous mercenary units, exercising with weapons, was a regular, repetitive part of every day. The primary weapons of the infantry were pikes and glaives, which showed up in Italy in
especially abundant forms.
Photo: Città del Grifo

DUKE SIGISMUND "THE RICH IN COIN" (*"der Münzreiche"*)

In the midst of the Alps lay the Princely County *(Gefürstete Grafschaft)* of Tirol. The Counts of Tirol originally had their domains in the Vinschgau.[18] From the Bishops of Brixen and Trient (Trento), the Counts acquired rights of a primary steward (*Kastvogteirechte*, Laten: *advocatus principalis*) which were rights to rule representing the ecclesiastic authorities. But soon the Tirolian Counts were exercising these rights primarily on their own authority and were rolling back the Bishops' political power and enlarging their territories at the Bishops' expense. A similar process (although with a different outcome) took place in western Tirol with regard to the Bishop of Chur. Count Albert III of Tirol and especially his grandson Count Meinhard II of Tirol-Görz[19] expanded their power and possessions through feuds, purchases and inheritances at the expense of other previously powerful noble families like the lords of Eppan or the lords of Wangen. For example, Count Meinhard II had already relatively realigned the borders of the domain. He also consolidated his rule of the regions internally. During his rule, the beginnings of a system of laws began, he fostered the development of a (by medieval standards) a strict administration and created offices with clear authorities. Additionally, he supported agriculture, he improved the legal status of the peasantry and furthered the emerging towns and cities. In doing so, he diminished the power of the local nobles. Country courts were established; princely judges and guardians concerned themselves with justice, taxes and defense. They had accounts due annually. In Tirol the princely power was asserted over the nobles quite early.

Count Meinhard II supported King Rudolf I of Habsburg, with whom he was closely allied since the Italian campaign, in the conflict with King Ottokar II of Bohemia and in return Meinhard was given the rank of an imperial prince in 1286[20] and awarded the Duchy of Carinthia (*Herzogtum Kärnten*). Along with that, marriage of their children was decided: Meinhard's daughter Elizabeth married Albrecht I, the German king from 1298 to 1308, and the couple became the progenitors of the later Habsburgs. Through this marriage, Tirol was to become a Habsburg inheritance in the future. In 1307, Meinhard's son Heinrich was chosen as the King of Bohemia and ruled Bohemia and Tirol in a personal union. But he only retained his rule of Bohemia until 1310. However, in Tirol he was able to further reduce the feudal authority of the Bishops of Trento and Brixen. After his death in 1335, his daughter Margarete[21] assumed rule of Tirol and in 1342 married Ludwig V of Bavaria from the House of Wittelsbach. Then when Ludwig V died in 1361, Margarete's soh, Meinhard III, took over the rule for two years. When he died in 1363 without an heir, Rudolf IV of the House of Habsburg became the Count of Tirol. As the Counts, the Habsburgs retained Tirol's independence. In the 1369 Treaty of Schärding the Wittelsbachs recognized Tirol as a Habsburg possession. And it was a valuable possession.

Tirol stretched to the south to Lake Garda and controlled the most important trade routes over the Alps. Every year, thousands of traders with their goods crossed through the Brenner, Arlberg and Resch Passes and enriched Tirol with transit duties. Furthermore, the country's mines produced immense profits. The silver mining in Schwaz provided a monetary blessing for the Tirolian princes' budget.[22] One of the most dazzling figures among Tirol's rulers was Duke Sigismund (Siegmund).

His pleasant-sounding cognomen – he was called "*der Münzreiche*" ("the Rich in Coin") – was based exclusively on his practice to have coins minted. Based on his (not atypical for the times) penchant for wasting money, he was chronically hard up.

This picture of Archduke Sigismund as a spendthrift and wannabe was considerably contributed by the French historian and diplomat Philippe de Commynes. In his memoires, which were considered a proper textbook for diplomacy and reached over 100 editions, Sigismund did not come away especially well. *"He was a man of little understanding and little honor; with such friends one finds little help. He was among the princes who did not want to know about their [the friends'] affairs other than what their servants chose to tell them."*

Initially all went well for the young duke from the Leopold family of the Habsburgs. His father, Frederick IV,[23] after a rough youth in poverty, Imperial ban and excommunication, succeeded in welding together the land of Tirol. Frederick's forces had defeated the noble opposition in the land or made it compliant and survived the conflict with the Swiss.[24] Additionally, his soldiers were in Trento, the city of the recalcitrant Archbishop Alexander

---

18   Area in the upper part of the Adige river valley in today's province of South Tirol, Italy.

19   Meinhard was born about 1239, *de jure* he was the Count of Tirol starting in 1258, de facto starting in 1259. He died on 30 October 1295 in Greifenburg.

20   Through this, the County of Tirol became an Imperial fief.

21   Also called "Margarete Maultasch," she was born in Tirol in 1318 and died on 3 October 1369 in Vienna.

22   The Count of Tirol's income around the mid-15th century was approximately 117,000 guilders. Other imperial princes came off more poorly, for example, the Duke of Saxony had an annual income of 39,000 guilders, the Margrave of Brandenburg got 33,000 guilders, the *Ezstift* (Archbishopric) of Cologne got 49,000 annually. Only the Electoral Prince of the Palatine (Pfalz) had a comparably high yearly income of about 100,000 guilders.

23   Friedrich IV, born in 1382; died 24 June 1439 in Innsbruck, Tirol.

24   This refers to the so-called "Appenzell Wars" ("*Appenzellerkriege*") of 1401 to 1429.

of Mazovia,[25] to put pressure on the ecclesiastic prince. The archbishop had attempted to befriend Milan and Venice and had brought about a bloody revolt by his subjects.

Furthermore, in the 1420s, one of the largest silver deposits in Europe was discovered on the so-called Falkenstein mountain in the Schwaz region. With this income and thanks to his solid commercial management, Duke Frederick[26] was able to successfully restructure and rise to being one of Europe's most powerful princes. In the period before his death, the County of Tirol experienced its height of power and prestige.

Archduke Sigismund of Tirol's coat of arms
Armorial of Hans Ulrich Fisch

In this safe world, Anna von Braunschweig-Göttingen,[27] Duke Frederick's second wife[28], gave birth to the long hoped-for heir on 26 October 1427. While the father busy conducting politics on a large scale, Siegmund (also called "Sigmund" or "Sigismund") grew up well-cared-for in the Neuhof (New Court), the princely residence in the heart of Innsbruck.

Little is known about Sigismund's childhood. It must certainly have been considerably different than that of his father Frederick. At the of age four, Frederick had lost his father, killed by the Swiss at the 1386 Battle of Sempach. From then on, Frederick had a hard struggle for his inheritance until he had finally overcome his last enemies.

Sigismund grew up in peaceful times and could use his father's considerable wealth to live a carefree life. There was even an official engagement of Sigismund to Princess Radegonde, the eldest daughter of the French King Charles VII. A bond with the Valois – the French royal house – could have had significant political results.

But soon the good life was over and the first of a series of unlucky calamities struck the young son of the prince: In 1439, Duke Frederick IV died in Innsbruck at barely 57 years old. He left his son a well-ordered country of Tirol with considerable revenues. But these riches immediately awoke the greed of Europe's powerful and Sigismund had the bad luck to have two powerful and unscrupulous cousins.[29]

The two Austrian Dukes Frederick V[30] and Albrecht VI[31] were nephews of Sigismund's father and only twelve and nine years older, respectively, than Sigismund. And they showed no scruples to, at least, temporarily get their young relative out of the way. Duke Frederick, the later king and emperor, as the eldest, took over guardianship of Sigismund. By doing that, he de facto took Tirol's rule and income and his brother Albrecht VI received the outlying Austrian lands.[32]

Under the pretext of better educating the young duke and preparing him to take over the rule, Frederick had him taken to Graz in Styria. The real reason was actually that Sigismund would be far from his hereditary lands and therefore had barely any influence. Beyond that, Frederick confiscated large portions of Tirol's considerable treas-

---

25 Also: Aleksander Mazowiecki; born 1400 in Płock, Poland; died 4 June 1444 in Vienna.

26 He was later called *"Friedl mit der leeren Tasche"* ("Freddy with the empty pockets") in the vernacular.

27 Born ca. 1390; died on 10 August 1432.

28 Frederick's first marriage was with Elisabeth von der Pfalz who died just two years after they married.

29 Compare Krones, Franz von, „Sigmund, Erzherzog von Oesterreich" in: *Allgemeine Deutsche Biographie*, published by der Historischen Kommission bei der Bayerischen Akademie der Wissenschaften, Band 34 (1892), pp. 286–294, specifically p. 286.

30 Later called Frederick III (Friedrich III) as Kaiser.

31 Born 18 December 1418 in Vienna; died 2 December 1463 there as well.

32 Those were the majority of Vorarlberg, the County of Pfirt (Ferrette), most of the Upper Alsace, the four forest cantons on the upper Rhine and the County of Hauenstein in the Southern Black Forest.

Flags of the most varied shape and style were important means of identification in which the individual commanders' and unit's power, reputation and respectability were visibly manifest for everyone. They frequently invoked heavenly powers with their words and pictures. In the confusion of battle they served as means to orient on the location of the commander or units. For the enemy they were coveted prizes that are often hung in churches and other public buildings.
Photo: Città del Grifo

Burg Sigmundskron, Illustration: Wolfgang Braun

ury, supposedly to keep it safe for Sigismund. Naturally these treasures would never go back to Tirol, plus Frederick could put the income to good use himself.

Sigismund was located far from the centers of power. Even though his cousin Frederick was essentially holding him prisoner in Graz, he enjoyed a comprehensive education. Among others, Enea Silvio Piccolomini, the later Pope Pius II, instructed him. He was, under Frederick III's instructions, supposed to have tried to convince the young duke choose a career in the Church because his high intellect should be used for higher callings. But Sigismund did not let this discourage him and when in 1443 he officially became an adult at the age of 16, he demanded to be released from guardianship.

However, he had the bad luck because Frederick was not planning to give up wealthy Tirol's incomes. Furthermore, he held the Tirolian Alpine passes, the shortest routes to the west and south. Meanwhile, in the west the "Old Zurich War" (1440-1446) was raging, in which the city of Zurich together with Duke Frederick of Austria was battling the other Swiss cantons. Using Sigismund's engagement to the French princess, King Frederick convinced the French crown to set in motion a mercenary army, the so-called "Armagnacs" against the Swiss. Despite the support of the nobles in the outlying lands, the Armagnacs were not able to decisively defeat the Swiss. In the exceptionally bloody 1444 battle of St. Jakob an der Birs,[33] the Swiss showed just what military achievements they were capable of, and the Armagnac Army withdrew. Afterward, the mercenary troops marauded for a few more months in Alsace, a large part of which belonged to the Habsburgs.

From Graz and Vienna, Sigismund tried to gain control in Tirol, but King Frederick stymied him again and again. When the Tirolian estates began to grumble because they were fed up with Frederick's strict rule, an unexpected message arrived from Vienna: Sigismund had agreed to an extension of the guardianship in July 1443, and for an additional six years! When one considers that before the signature, Sigismund had tried everything to avoid exactly that, one must conclude that it did not happen voluntarily. He was probably forced into it by Frederick.

It did not take long before there were protests from Tirol. A group of nobles gathered around Oswald von Wolkenstein,[34] the famous minstrel (*Minnesänger*) and his brother Theobald, who denounced allegiance to King Frederick in his function as the Count of Tirol. They organized a congress (*Landtag*) in Meran to which Duke Sigismund was also invited, but whose attendance the King knew to prevent. At the *Landtag* the estates agreed to

---

33 If the French crown had ever planned that, supposedly the King and Dauphin at least want to get control of the Bishopric of Basel and of Alsace.

34 He was born around 1377, supposedly in the Schöneck Castle in the Puster Valley in South Tirol; died on 2 August 1445 in Meran.

stop paying any more taxes to the King until he released Sigismund. Additionally, they secured the borders to defend against a military blow by Frederick. Towns that did not agree with this tough approach went to rack and ruin. In the course of this, the Tirolian army captured the town of Trento.

Meanwhile, in the "Old Zurich War" a defeat was looming for King Frederick – a relief of the city by the Armagnacs did not materialize. In order to at least bring the insubordinate Tirolians under control, Frederick wanted to cede the rule to Sigismund but not without blackmailing him again: in February 1445, young Sigismund had to yield to his cousin the fiefs of Laxenburg, Mödling, Starhemberg and Wartenstein with nothing in return. In addition, after taking over rule of Tirol, he was supposed to always be at Frederick's service and get his concurrence on political decisions. The outlying Austrian lands remained in Albrecht VI's hands, initially for a period of six years. For this, Sigismund obligated himself to pay his cousin 20,000 guilders per year in order to finance his war against the Swiss.

Relying on his Tirolian subjects as well as Charles VII, the Kingof France and his future father-in-law, he accepted these harsh conditions. But he hoped that as an independent prince he could improve the nearly degrading conditions. Yet in this tense situation, bad luck still followed the Duke: in March 1445, Princess Radegonde of France died during the preparations for the wedding. That not only prevented Sigismund's leap to Europe's political elite, but also a certain independence from his Habsburg relatives by a close tie with France.

It was the Tirolian estates who dared with their threat to take up armed struggle against Dukes Frederick and Albrecht that forced Sigismund release from captivity on 9 April 1446.

On 28 April 1446, he was able to enter Tirol as the land's ruler. Despite the heavy payments to his two cousins Frederick and Albrecht, the prince was able to spend a large sum because of impressive incomes. Initially everything went splendidly. Thanks to the support from the Tirolian *Landestag*, Sigismund succeeded in modernizing the administration, improving the roads used for trade, and above all to accelerate the silver mining in Schwaz. For example, from 1447 to 1449 he saw the creation of the Mining Rules of Schwaz ("*Schwazer Bergordnung*"), that would be model for all of Europe and the New World.

After the untimely death of his promised bride, Sigismund started the search for a new candidate for marriage. Through the good offices of friendly nobles at the French Court, a marriage was arranged with Eleonore,[35] the daughter of the Scottish king. With Eleonore, Sigismund had an active and self-confident woman at his side. She was highly educated, active in literary circles, and when Sigismund was away sporadically, she ruled Tirol alone.

---

35 She was born ca. 1433 in Dunfermline, Scotland.

The Gradner Brothers

When Duke Sigismund entered Innsbruck in 1448, he brought with him the brothers VBG, knights from Styria. The two were highly regarded by the young duke, who soon made them his advisors. He showered the two with demonstrations of favor, including even reverted liens, like the Lichtenberg Castle in the Vinschgau. In 1449, Bernhard Gradner married Veronica, the only child of Ulrich von Starkenberg. He had been a leader of the nobles' *fronde* with his brother Wilhelm against the former Duke of Tirol. Sigismund had taken Wilhelm back into grace, and he had declared Veronica as the heiress to Ulrich – whose fate is unclear but was declared dead in 1430.

In 1451 Sigismund borrowed the considerable sum of 24,000 guilders from Bernhard Gradner, whom he had made the marshal of the court in the meantime. In 1453 the Pietra and Beseno Castles went over to the Gradner brothers as liens from the Bishopric of Trento at Duke Sigismund's instigation. Sigismund's cousin, Albrecht, began to make serious accusations against the Gradners. He was supported in this by Sigismund's other advisors, especially by Ulrich von Matsch. Both Gradners were removed from their offices and in January 1456 expelled from the country. While Vigilius and Bernhard's wife Veronica went to the Swiss Confederation, Bernhard thought he could hold out in his strong Beseno Castle. The Trento Bishop's forces besieged the castle for weeks in the summer of 1456 until Bernhard finally gave up and likewise went to the Swiss Confederation.

From: Jäger, Albert, "Die Fehde der Brüder Vigilius und Bernhard Gradner gegen Herzog Sigmund von Tirol", in: *Denkschriften der kaiserlichen Akademie der Wissenschaften* (Vienna: Kaiserlich-Königlichen Hof- und Staatsdruckerei, 1859), pp. 233–301.

Armored cavalry still played an important role in armies around 1480.
Illustration: Sascha Lunyakov

The couple's childlessness presented a great misfortune politically speaking. This may not have been Sigismund's fault, given that the Duke did not exactly follow rules of marital fidelity. In the course of the years, he produced at least forty illegitimate children, estimates even go as high as sixty, but some of these claims must certainly have been spurious since it was sufficiently well-known that the Duke took financially good care of these "love children".

Sigismund's relationship with Duke Albrecht VI was mostly friendly. Up until 1464, he obtained the outlying lands from Albrecht in competition with Frederick III, through purchases (in 1458 the Margraveship of Burgau[36] among others) and managing of inheritances.[37] To go along with the acquisition of these regions, Sigismund's policies gradually intensified toward the west; they were aimed at limiting the power of the neighboring Swiss, the Habsburgs' traditional opponents, winning back the former Habsburg regions previously lost to the Swiss starting in 1415 and not lastly, the creation of a land bridge from the Arlberg region to Alsace.

Sigismund came into direct conflict with the Swiss Confederation in 1458 in the so-called "*Plappartkrieg*" when Swiss forces occupied the town of Rapperswil, an important cornerstone in this region. However, Sigismund did not proceed by going to war, but intervened with Pope Pius II. Pope Pius II was no one other than Sigismund's old teacher in Graz: Enea Silvio Piccolomini, who had once unsuccessfully tried to force the young Sigismund into the life of a cleric. The Pope threaten the Swiss with excommunication if they did not give back the town. Later the Holy Father changed his mind and ordered the Swiss to occupy Habsburg territories in the name of the Lord.

Along with the continuing conflicts with the Swiss, Sigismund had the misfortune of becoming the enemy of the new Prince-Bishop of Brixen. The new bishop was none other than Cardinal Nikolaus von Kues, better known as Nicolaus Cusanus[38] (1401–1464). Cusanus is known today as one of the leading spiritual greats of the Middle Ages. Besides his spiritual tracts in philosophy, mathematics and theology, the new bishop stood out because of his excellent relationship with the Pope.

As an enlightened theologian, Cusanus attempted to use his theories for a reform of the practice of Christianity. In doing so, he came into conflict with Duke Sigismund, who denounced his wild lifestyle. Furthermore, Cusanus wanted to bring Tirol's de-facto independent monasteries back under the authority of the diocese. In the argument about the rights of the Sonnenburg Monastery in the Puster Valley, the conflict degenerated into violence. In the 1458 "Battle in the Enne Mountains" ("*Schlacht im Enneberg*"), the Tirolian farmers defeated the Bishop's mercenaries and killed fifty of them.

The Bishop did not let that discourage him and continued to taunt Sigismund. It even went so far as Cusanus barricading himself in the town of Bruneck's castle and the Duke besieging the town in 1460. Sigismund's forces rapidly succeeded in overcoming the walls and capturing the obstinate Bishop. Despite the subsequent peace treaty, Cusanus made his way to Rome where he effected Sigismund's and the land of Tirol's excommunication by his friend, Pope Pius II.

This decree of excommunication led to the Swiss Confederation feeling obliged to declare war on Sigismund. Gradually many of the Confederation's town denounced the Duke and marched against Diessenhofen and Winterthur. Duke Sigismund was not able to raise an army that was able to stand up to the enemy, and so Diessenhofen fell, while Winterthur remained in Habsburg hands until 1467. As a result, the former Austrian Thurgau region was completely lost to the Swiss Confederation.[39]

Meanwhile, the Duke's private life did not appear very rosy. In spite of his early, immense wealth, he piled up gigantic debts. Around the turn of the years 1478-79, Sigismund had a net annual income of a formidable 104,082 guilders. Of that, the lion share of 79,440 guilders was from sales from the silver production in the Inn Valley. The balance came from tolls and offices whereby, however, the majority of the incomes were already obligated. Sigismund maintained an exceptionally wasteful court: his father had been satisfied with a small court of barely 100 people in the old residence in Innsbruck. Sigismund, for his purposes, had a new court castle built, and by 1490 his retinue had grown to 500 people. The Duke was markedly jovial and credulous. Many shady characters exploited this shamelessly and enriched themselves at the Duke's expense.

Besides that, the Duke carried out an extensive construction program and among other things, had seven hunting palaces built. These had ostentatious names like "Sigismund's Desire" ("Sigmundslust"), "Sigismund's Rest" ("Sigmundsruh"), "Sigismund's Castle" ("Sigmundsburg"), "Sigismund's Corner" ("Sigmundsegg") and "Sigismund's Peace" ("Sigmundsfried"). "Sigismund's Crown" ("Sigmundskron" or "Siegmundskron"), near Bolzano

---

36 See Jedelhauser, Philipp, *Beiträge zum Beginn und zum Ende der Herrschaft der Markgrafen von Burgau aus dem Hause Berg*, 2. überarbeitete Auflage (2nd revised edition) (Krumbach: Frick, 2017), pp. 4–5.

37 While Sigismund supported the Wittelsbach Dukes of the Palatine (Pfalz) of Bavaria-Landshut against Kaiser Frederick III in the Margraves' War, Duke Albrecht actually attacked his imperial brother militarily. Also see Gismann, Robert, *Die Beziehungen zwischen Tirol und Bayern im Ausgang des Mittelalters, Herzog Siegmund der Münzreiche und die Wittelsbacher in Landshut und München von 1439–1479* (Innsbruck: Universität Innsbruck, 1976).

38 Born in 1401 in Kues on the Moselle, today Bernkastel-Kues; died 11 August 1464 in Todi, Umbria.

39 Also the Gradner brothers (Vigilius and Bernhard), recent citizens of Zurich, did what they could to incite the Swiss Confederates to fight against Duke Sigismund.

(German: Bozen) with its exceptionally massive fortress complex, was among the Duke's constructs. Around 1473, the Duke purchased the castle and named it "Our Castle Sigismund's Crown" (1474: "*unser slosz Sigmundskron*"[40]). Also, the Duke owned many castles that were actually outside of Tirol.[41]

Even rich Tirol could not afford these enormous expenses and because Sigismund did not have very good luck with financial matters, he gradually mortgaged the greater part of his territories, especially in the Austrian Outlands. Additionally, there were repeated military conflicts with the Swiss which often Sigismund did not initiate but resulted from nobles in the Outlands who were happy to feud.

In 1468 the Free Imperial City of Mülhausen in Alsace (now Mulhouse, France) declared hostilities against Duke Sigismund of Tirol after it had already been in conflict for a long time with neighboring Upper Alsatian nobles (in the so-called "Six Plappert War" – "*Sechsplappertkrieg*" of 1465-66).[42] After a minor military success by the Bernese in the Sundgau (in Alsace), the other Swiss Confederates advanced and besieged the Habsburg town of Waldshut in the summer of 1468 (the siege began on 29 July).[43] The Bernese, Freiburg (in Uechland) and Solothurn forces joined them but could not take the town which was defended by Bilgeri von Heudorf and Wernher von Schinen. It was their own fault. Despite the brave defense by the Waldshut guilds, the town would certainly have fallen if the besieging Swiss army had not been overcome by disunity about how to proceed. Some Swiss cantons would have been too happy to see the Black Forest communities join the Confederation. At least they were trying to have good relations. And that must have been exactly what was worrying Duke Sigismund. Sigismund's influential counselors were afraid of losing the towns in the Black Forest to the Swiss Confederation. The Duke could not relieve the town by himself. The suggestion to entrust the Waldhut's relief to the Palatine Electoral Prince Friedrich, one of the most successful and uncompromising commanders among the imperial princes, got of all things, no concurrences.[44] Then Duke Sigismund began peace negotiations with the Swiss.

A peace treaty (the so-called "*Waldshuter Richtung*") was achieved on 27 August 1468. It agreed to Sigismund having to pay a transfer fee of 10,000 Rhenish guilders to the Swiss and until it was paid, Waldshut and the Black Forest would be relinquished to them collateral. On 26 May 1469, Emperor Frederick III, Sigismund's domineering cousin, declared the treaty as invalid and issued a "ban of the Empire "*Reichsacht*" on the Swiss which had no further results. However, Sigismund of Tirol, because of his extravagant management of his court, could not come up with the 10,000 guilders being demanded. Therefore, he finally turned to France's King Louis XI who rebuffed him, before he asked for help from the wealthy and ambitious Burgundian Duke Charles the Bold. Charles had the 10,000-guider debt paid to the Swiss. Furthermore, on 5 September 1469 he concluded the Treaty of St. Omer. Duke Charles paid the Tirolean Duke 50,000 guilders and received the County of Pfirt (now Ferrette, France), the rural County of Upper Alsace, the Black Forest, the four "Forest Communities (*Waldstätte*) on the Rhine and Breisach as liens.[45] He also committed to side with Sigismund against the Swiss. In 1469 the Duke sought out the Burgundian Duke Charles at the Prinsenhof palace in Bruges to speak with him about the prospect of a Burgundian-Habsburg marriage. But Duke Charles' answer remained vague.

Duke Sigismund leases the Alsace to Duke Charles the Bold, from Diebold Schilling's Chronicle.
Facsimile from the original manuscript

---

40 Quoted from Obermair, Hannes, *Schriftlichkeit und urkundliche Überlieferung der Stadt Bozen bis 1500; in: Bozen Süd–Bolzano Nord. Band 2* (Bolzano: LIT, 2008), p. 156.

41 Sigimund had a weakness for luxurious properties. In 1462 he acquired the badly damaged Hohkönigsburg (Haut Koenigsbourg) in Alsace in a punitive action against some robber barons. See Strobel, Adam Walther, *Die Vaterländische Geschichte des Elsasses von der frühesten bis auf die gegenwärtige Zeit, Dritter Teil* (Straßburg: Schmidt und Grucker, 1843), p. 380.

42 Seehase, Hagen and Ollesch, Detlef, *Kurfürst Friedrich der Siegreiche von der Pfalz (1425–1476)* (Petersberg: Imhof, 2013), pp. 76–79.

43 See: Hansjakob, Heinrich, *Der Waldshuter Krieg vom Jahre 1468* (Waldshut: H. Zimmermann, 1868), p. 30.

44 If Prince Friedrich had simply wanted to, he could have had very good relations with the Swiss.

45 Duke Sigismund spent the money very quickly. On 31 August 1474 he purchased the County of Sonnenberg for 34,000 guilders from Count Graf Eberhard I. In 1472, Eberhard's son, Andreas von Sonnenberg, had injured a citizen of Bludenz (Austria) and Duke Sigismund of Tirol's subject, so it resulted in a conflict that the Duke exploited in order to have mercenaries from Feldkirch (Switzerland) under Burkhard von Knöringen capture and then destroy the Sonnenberg Castle after a three-day siege in 1473. The last money from this sale in 1474 was finally received many years later by Eberhard's heir George III of Waldburg-Zeil.

The captain of this group of mercenaries has removed most of his plate armor for training exercises.
The cloth protective wams, which forms the innermost layer of the armor, is visible. It is covered with chainmail on the shoulders, upper arms and armpits, in order to close the gaps in the armor that are needed for movement. Also the lower torso is covered with a surrounding chainmail skirt.
Photo: Città del Grifo

Sigismund shortly regretted having leased most of the Outlands. Some of the nobles there began to come to terms with the Burgundian rule. However, the Burgundian steward, named Peter von Hagenbach, started to butt heads with the local notables. [46] At the end of August 1472, Duke Sigismund negotiated with representatives of the Swiss Confederation, but then received a delegation from the Duke of Burgundy with Hagenbach as its head. In 1474, Duke Sigismund pressed Charles to renew hostilities against the Swiss, but again Charles refused. When it was finally clear to Sigismund that the Duke of Burgundy would not engage in his plans against the Swiss, he did a radical about face and attempted to join with the Confederation. Initially they established the important alliance with the "Lower Union" ("*Niedere Vereinigung*"), an alliance of the imperial cities of Basel, Kolmar (Colmar), Schlettstadt (now Sélestat, France) and Strasbourg. Thanks to King Louis XI, the "Perpetual Accord" ("*Ewige Richtung*") with Duke Sigismund came into existence on 30 March 1474. The Bishop of Constance, Hermann von Breitenlandenberg, who in 1468 had already negotiated between the Swiss and the Tirolean Duke, decisively helped shape the agreement. In the Perpetual Accord, Sigismund renounced all claims to territories inside the Swiss Confederation and recognized it as independent from Habsburg rule. In return the Swiss promised to never touch the Habsburg lands on the other side of the border. Then Sigismund notified Duke Charles he was terminating the lease contract. The Alsatian towns had paid 80,000 guilders for the termination of the same thing. However, Duke Charles refused to accept the notification of the termination of the Treaty of St. Omer, he had even invested an additional 170,000 guilders (according to his own statements) in the leased lands. [47] In April

---

46 Also called Pierre de Hagenbach, he was an Alsatian-Burgundian noble. See also Brauer-Gramm, Hildburg, *Der Landvogt Peter von Hagenbach–Die burgundische Herrschaft am Oberrhein 1469–1474* (Göttingen: Duehrkohp & Radicke, 2001), 2001).

47 Parts of the region had already been leased by Duke Sigismund to other nobles and towns in previous years. The Duke of Burgundy had had to gradually take over these lease payments in order to get control of these locations, e.g., over the commune of Thann that had been leased to Heinrich Reich von Reichenstein.

Castel Beseno, Photo: Florian Messner

1474, a revolt against Hagenbach began in the leased lands, so Sigismund immediately grasped the opportunity to take possession of them. [48] In the subsequent Burgundian Wars, which led to the defeat of the duchy and Duke Charles' death, the Swiss formed the militarily most significant part of the anti-Burgundian alliance. But the driving political forces were the French crown and the imperial cities, along with Duke Sigismund because Charles the Bold's death was to his advantage. Some of Sigismund's vassals and servants distinguished themselves in the fighting against the Burgundians. Among them, for example, was Friedrich Kappler from the Alsace. In 1476, Sigismund released those subjects of the various nobles and clerics who the lords had obtained in the past as inherited serfs ("*Eigenlueute*"), namely the Augsburg, Babenberg and Hilpold people and he personally relinquished receiving life-long annuities. Those who had been freed from the status of bondage were supposed to pay taxes and be liable for military service in the jurisdictions where they lived. [49]

In 1477 Sigismund was elevated to the rank of arch duke which did little for him politically, but which necessitated him maintaining an even more costly court. He maintained the peace with the Swiss whose victories over the Burgundians had brought them tremendous wealth and respect – and they kept the peace them with him. With the Treaty of Stans ("*Stanser Verkommnis*") of December 1481 the Swiss Confederation consolidated itself internally. The conflict between the rural and urban cantons had among other things, raised the question of whether to admit Freiburg (Fribourg) and Solothurn into the Confederation. Dividing up the spoils from the Burgundian Wars also played a big role. The conflict was resolved after

---

48 See Ollesch, Detlef and Seehase, Hagen, *The Burgundian Wars*, (Berlin: Zeughaus, 2019, p. 22.

49 In Tirol from then on, personal bondage was no longer widespread, around 1520 three nobility families (Trapp, Thun and the Schrofensteiners) still held bonded people (*Eigenleute*). But along with that there were still the rural bonded people of Imst who were finally freed in the second half of the 16th century.

tough negotiations[50] and the agreement[51] (prohibition of military actions against other confederates, commitment to provide military assistance in case of an attack, etc.) strengthened the Confederation significantly. Swiss mercenaries were now more sought after abroad than ever before, not only in France, but also by the Habsburgs.

Archduke Sigismund became increasingly senile and came under the influence of self-serving advisors. It was due in part to the death of his wife Eleonore in 1480 who had played a moderating role in his life. Then Archduke Sigismund started searching for a new wife who could bear him the desired heir. He chose the 16-year-old Catherine (Katharina) of Saxony,[52] forty-one years younger than her future husband. But even after the wedding in 1484 no children were born and thus no heir to the land of Tirol.

Sigismund cultivated an increasingly close relationship with the Duke of Bavaria Munich, Albrecht IV. In 1467 he had rejected a request for assistance from his brother, Duke Christoph the Strong, who was eager for a fight against Albrecht. Kaiser Frederick III, facing the Hungarian threat to Vienna and the eastern part of Austria, had taken his daughter Kunigunde to Innsbruck where she could remain safely and, in a manner befitting her social status. Duke Albrecht IV visited there now and then and in 1485 met Kunigunde. The charming, but 18 year older, Albrecht imagined a marriage to Kunigunde would increase his power. Frederick III, for his part, who was always short of funds, was hoping to get help from the quite wealthy Albrecht. He agreed to the betrothal. Furthermore, Kunigunde was supposed to receive a 20,000-guilder dowry, to which Archduke Sigismund wanted to add 40,000.[53]

During the marriage negotiations Albrecht still occupied the imperial city of Regensburg. Additionally, the Emperor withdrew his approval of the marriage. Albrecht, with help from Sigismund, presented Kunigunde with a forged approval from the Emperor, so the wedding took place on 2 January, 1487 in the castle chapel in Innsbruck.[54] Shortly after Three Kings Day [6 January?] the couple left Innsbruck and a little later entered Munich very ceremoniously and with many followers and servants. The Emperor was infuriated when he got word about it. He probably would have been even more angry if he had recognized the full scope of the Bavarian influence in Tirol. Duke Albrecht IV had infiltrated Sigismund's court with people loyal to himself and was getting accurate reports on what was happening in the Innsbruck court.

Thomas Pipperle, Duke Albrecht IV von Bayern-München's servant and chamberlain (and possibly the Forester of Tölz in Upper Bavaria), was an important intermediary in Duke Albrecht's reconciliation with Archduke Sigismund of Tirol. He was often employed as a messenger between the two courts and enjoyed the complete trust of his master. Around the turn of the year 1486-87, he was in the service of Archduke Sigismund. Anna Spiess,[55] written as "Spiessin" in the early form, was the widow of the court knight Leopold Spiess von Friedberg. A chronicle describes her in a not very flattering way as a "tall and gaunt woman, not pleasant in body or spirit" (*groz und hager weip, nit angenehm an koerper und geist*"). She was one of Archduke Sigismund's former lovers and was in correspondence with Albrecht IV. At the beginning of 1487, she was accused of witchcraft, supposedly having harmed four women with magic. But she escaped judgement by fleeing.

Along with the Bavarian faction at the Innsbruck court, there was also a small Saxon one consisting of servants who had accompanied Katherina of Saxony to Innsbruck. They arrived in Tirol not to oppose the influential counselors, but to ensure that the Emperor would stay informed about the machinations of the pro-Bavarian party. The so-called "Poisoning Affair" ("*Vergiftungsaffäre*") was an intrigue like out of a drama: Sigismund's Master of the Kitchen, Matthias Rainer, just happened to have read a letter, which Anna Spiess had written to Duke Albrecht IV in Munich. In it, Anna Spiess notified him that Sigismund's young wife intended to poison Sigismund. And then she wanted, with help from her father, Duke Albrecht of Saxony, to seize power in Tirol, drown Anna Spiess and have the Counts of Werdenberg and Matsch beheaded. Behind the plan for the poisoning stood none other than Duke Albrecht of Saxony and the Emperor himself. The Master of the Kitchen, Rainer, informed the Saxon Duke and also Emperor Frederick III. But more important than the "Poisoning Affair" was Sigismund's decision, supposedly or actually based on the disastrous influence of the counselors mentioned, to raise money – lots of money – from the Bavarian Dukes.

---

50 According to tradition, the negotiating parties only came to an agreement after the intervention of the hermit Niklaus von Flüe (1417 to 1487).

51 Plus, it included the agreement to divide wartime booty according to the number of individuals from a canton who participated in a campaign, and conquered lands were to be given to the cantons in equal parts.

52 Katharina was the eldest child of Duke Albrecht the Courageous (*der Beherzte*) of Saxony and his wife Sidonie of Bohemia. She was born on 24 July 1468 in Grimma, Saxony; died on 10 February 1524 in Calenberg

53 See Prokop Freiherr von Freyberg, Maximilian, *Pragmatische Geschichte der bayerischen Gesetzgebung und Staatsverwaltung seit den Zeiten Maximilian I.* (Leipzig: Friedrich Fleischer, 1839), p. 177.

54 See Wolf, Susanne, *Die Doppelregierung Kaiser Friedrich III. und König Maximilian (1487–1493)* (Cologne, Weimar and Vienna: Böhlau, 2005), p. 460.

55 In earlier written form she appears as "Anna Spiessin".

THE *GUERRA RETICA* AND ITS CAUSES

The "Venetian War" of 1487 is also known sometimes as the "Rovereto War" or in Italian as the "*Guerra Retica.*" Just as little as a commonly accepted designation has taken hold, are historians in agreement over the causes for the war. Sometimes the maritime Venetian Republic's expansionist and exploiting policies are cited, sometimes, the Venetian War is seen as a shortsighted adventure driven by the irresponsible (and greedy) counselors of the somewhat senile Archduke. The war was not in the Tiroleans interest, who received many goods via Venice and whose merchants could profit considerably from transit taxes. The Venetians for their part were very interested in a stable situation in the trade routes that passed through Tirol to their customers north of the Alps.

In the past decades, there had been frequent conflicts over Trento between the Republic and the Duchy. In the 14th century, the Liechtenstein-Kastelkorn families provided ministers to the bishops of Trento and the counts of Tirol. In 1390 a member of the house, George I von Liechtenstein, became the Bishop of Trento. He was selected by the cathedral chapter as the Bishop of Trento with the support of Duke Albrecht III. Because the vote took place at the time of the "Great Schism," it was confirmed by the Roman line of the Papacy (Boniface IX). John XXIII (Pisan line) rejected him as a cardinal. Bishop George frequently was in conflict with Duke Frederick IV of Tirol. But he was also having disagreements with Trento's citizenry. Trento's citizens were especially aggravated about the bishopric's vicar who was responsible for the city. On 2 February 1407, enraged masses, under the leadership of the nobleman Negro de' Negri di Santo Pietro, marched on the Pretorio Palace in Trento and protested against the repressive tax burden, and demanded the dismissal of the hated vicar. The Bishop, holed up in the Buonconsiglio Castle, was surprised by the unrest. Over the course of the month, the Bishop felt forced to make far-reaching concessions and to give up authorities. On 28 February 1407, he eventually signed the so-called "*Magna Charta Libertatum Tridenti*" (Great Charter of Liberty of Trento") in which he agreed to, among other things, the election of the city council, control over the city vicar's official activities, and the naming of a so-called Captain of the People. Rodolfo Belenzani, who had not yet appeared during the rebellion, was entrusted with the role of the Captain. But Bishop George soon regretted the concessions he had made, and he sought help from the Condottiere Ottobono da Parma, who was in the service of the Duke of Milan, to put down militarily the rebellion. The appeal for help did not go unnoticed and Belenzani then tried for his part to dispose of the Bishop, in which Count Frederick IV of Tirol supported him. When the Bishop refused to hand over the Buonconsiglio Castle, he had him locked up in the Vanga Tower on 4 April 1407.

When, a few days later, after the Bishop's properties had been plundered, Rodolfo asked the Count of Tirol for assistance to quell any further unrest. Shortly thereafter, on 16 April 1407, Tirolean forces, under the leadership of Heinrich VI von Rottenberg, occupied the city. In the meantime, Belenzani with his men besieged the Pergine Castle that was held by subjects loyal to the Bishop. Initially Frederick IV guaranteed the town additional rights, thereby completely ignoring the Bishop. For his services, Belenzani was promised to receive fiefs as well as titles as a captain and a mayor. With the help of several lawyers from Padua, who were his friends, Rodolfo worked out a statute for the town that served as a model for other community statutes in the principality. The Bishop, who was forced to side, refused any cooperation in the face of the new conditions and was first put under house arrest before he left, more or less fled in July 1407, in the direction of Vienna, from where he finally returned at the end of 1409. The harmony between Frederick IV and the anti-Bishop movement ended relatively quickly. The Duke occupied important positions with his followers, which finally led to open opposition by Belenzani and his adherents. On 6 October 1407, Belenzani was arrested by Frederick IV's people, the Captain's Office was disbanded, and the granted privileges partially canceled. Belenzani avoided imprisonment because a friend paid a bail of 25,000 ducats. But instead of appearing before he Duke as imposed, he fled and sought new allies that he appears to have arranged in the Venetian Republic. In the Venetian-held town of Rovereto (German: Rofreit) he gathered a group of armed men. Also, some castellans, like Negro de' Negri in Stenico were opposed to the new order. However, Venice held back from a formal alliance, not trusting the rebels and not wanting to risk its considerable economic with the Tiroleans. Left on his own, Belenzani moved with his followers toward Trento on 28 June 1409. The Duke's followers, after some of them had been killed by the rebels, pulled back into the Buonconsiglio Castle (Castello di Buonconsiglio), which Rodolfo Belenzani then besieged. Frederick IV's answer did not take long, and on 5 July his forces retook the town. In that bloody engagement between the Tiroleans and the rebels, Rodolfo Belenzani was fatally wounded and died the same day. [56]

The Tirolean Kastelwarg[57] family was also involved in the conflict. When a renewed rebellion against the Bishop broke out in May 1410, Heinrich VI von Rottenburg attacked Trento and had the town horribly laid waste. The Duke Friedrich rushed there and Rottenburgs retreated to Bavaria, and Bishop George to Vienna. When the Duke was put under and Imperial ban, the Bishop was able, *pro*

---

[56] In the older depictions an execution is mentioned.

[57] The Italian name Castelbarco has become common and will be used henceforth.

forma with Emperor Sigismund's help, to regain control of this seat. But these rights could not be carried out and George III returned to Trento shortly before his death in 1419.

By 1303 the Beseno Castle, the strongest complex in Tyrol, had fallen to the Castelbarco lords (Italian for Kastelwarg). The Castelbarcos were in constant feuds with the neighboring noble houses, the lords of Arco and the lords of Lodron, whereby they were supported in changing alliances sometimes with the Bishopric of Trento, sometimes with the County of Tirol, and from time to time with Venice. In 1416 the Venetians destroyed several castles belonging to the Castelbarcos. When a defeat of the Castelbarcos loomed, they turned to the Duke of Tirol. Also, that same year Duke Frederick IV received a promise of the town and castle of Rovereto through a settlement with Aldrigeso da Castelbarco.[58] However, the Venetians presented a fact: after a one-week siege they captured the Rovereto Castle. And they had come to stay. The Pietra di Calliano Castle was a (feudal) possession of the Castelbarcos.[59] Marcobrun da Castelbarco, the last in this line of the family, had no heirs. His castles of Beseno and Pietra were transferred during his lifetime as fiefdoms of the Trento Bishopric to the Tirolean Counsels Vigilius and Bernhard Gradner.[60] The Bishop of Trento and also Duke Sigismund of Tirol feared (not completely without cause), that these key positions in the Adige (German: Etsch) Valley could fall to the Venetians.[61]

An important regional power factor was the Lodron family, which was originally from the culturally Italian area. The brothers Giorgio and Pietro helped their family, through skilled alliances, efficient administration of their lands and military successes as commanders in the pay of foreigners, to a significant ascendance. In 1452, Emperor Frederick III raised the two brothers to the rank of Imperial Counts of Castelromano and Lodron. In 1456, the Prince-Bishop of Trent, George II, Hack von Themeswald,[62] tasked the brothers Giorgio and Pietro Lodron to seize the castles of Castelnuovo, Castellano, Nomi and Castelcorno from the Counts of Castelbarco, who did not recognize the Prince-Bishop as their lord. In 1460 the Castello di Tenno on the north shore of Lake Garda again came under the control of the Bishop of Trento. Bishop George III died in 1465. In August 1465, Johannes Hinderbach, a confidant of Emperor Frederick III was chosen as the Prince-Bishop of Trento and on 12 May 1466 his nomination was confirmed by Pope Paul II.

One of the most significant nobles of the region was Francesco d´Arco.[63] It was always important for him to be considered as a vassal of the Holy Roman Empire. When his brother Galeazzo intrigued against him, he had him imprisoned. Count Francesco died in 1482. Francesco d´Arco left behind three sons, Andrea, Camillo und Odorico.[64] Camillo, who was led astray by his uncle Galeazzo D'Arco's enticements, definitely had a part in the conspiracy, but he fled and only returned after his father's death. Then his trail disappeared: whether he, as sometimes claimed, became a robber, or whether he turned to the Venetians for help, is uncertain.[65] Odorico d'Arco married the Venetian noblewoman Susanna Collalto. That was not only a social event of the greatest significance, but also would also have political consequences.

In 1486 the Prince-Bishop Johannes Hinderbach, as a result of the conflict between Duke Sigismund of Tirol and the Venetians, was sent to the Signoria and died shortly after his return (21 September).[66]

In the winter of 1486-1487, the situation intensified because the death of the Prince-Bishop of Trento, Johannes Hinderbach left a power vacuum that the local nobles tried to exploit in order to realize claims to territories. On 30 September 1486, Trento's Cathedral Chapter elected Ulrich on Frundsberg[67] as bishop, but the papal confirmation was still missing, so his position was still not confirmed.

The County (*Grafschaft*) of Görz lay on the border between the County of Tirol and the Venetian Republic. In 1460, the young count Johann Heinrich – without the concurrence of Görz's estates – started the Cillian War of Succession.[68] Some of the Görz nobles, who also had Austrian fiefs, refused to fight against the Emperor. The young

---

58 See Brandis, Clemens Wenzeslaus, *Graf zu: Tirol unter Friedrich von Österreich* (Vienna: Franz Ludwig, 1821), pp. 15–16.

59 See Bidermann, Hermann Ignaz, *Die Italiäner im Tirolischen Provinzial-Verbande* (Innsbruck: Wagner, 1874), p. 6.

60 Marcobrun von Castlebarco received the right to dwell there and could also collect incomes from the lands belonging to them.

61 See Jäger, Albert "Die Fehde der Brüder Vigilius und Bernhard Gradner gegen Herzog Sigmund von Tirol," in *Denkschriften der kaiserlichen Akademie der Wissenschaften* (Vienna: K.K. Hof- und Staatsdruckerei, 1859), pp. 233–301, specifically p. 241.

62 The Hack originally came from Silesia.

63 According to the family's own passed down records, it originated in Bavaria. Francesco was born in 1413 as the son of Antonio, *Conte* (Count) d'Arco and Angelica Nogarola; he married Francesca Pellegrini and in 1433 was declared the sole heir. Francesco wanted to share power with his brother Galeazzo, but the latter tried to depose him. Therefore, Francesco imprisoned his brother for the remainder of his life (for at least 26 years). He then was a captain in Sienna, died in 1482 and had the following children: his heir Andrea (1434 -1507), Odorico d' Arco, Camillo d´Arco, Filippa, Bartolomea, Angela and Pacifica.

64 It is also spelled "Udalrico" and Ulrich".

65 See Perini, Agostino, *I castelli del Tirolo*, Vol. 2 (Milano: Pirotta, 1839), p. 76.

66 See Krones, Franz von, "Johannes Hinderbach" in *Allgemeine Deutsche Biographie*, published by the *Historischen Kommission* of the Bayerischen Akademie der Wissenschaften, Band 12 (Bavarian Academy of Science, Vol. 12) (1880), pp. 457–458, specifically p. 458.

67 He was an older brother of the famous *Landsknecht* leader Georg von Frundsberg.

68 The war was started by the murder of the last count of Cilli, Ulrich II, on 8 November 1456 in Belgrade.

Thurgau pikemen
depicted by the reenactment group Arma Georgii
Photo Fred Wutz

count, who had completely overestimated his strength, suffered a mortifying defeat. He had certainly hoped to expand his Carinthian domains, but now lost everything that his family had acquired in Carinthia over the past 400 years, even the family's cloister of Millstatt. He could be happy that he was able to at least retain dominion of Lienz.[69]

Heavily armored soldier with an open helmet in the Tiroleans' army.
Photo: Condottieri Maurizani

The entire reign of his successor Count Leonhard was shaped by efforts to regain the Carinthian possessions lost in 1460. He joined changing coalitions with the Emperor's opponents: Albrecht VI, Sigismund of Tirol[70] and even King Matthias Corvinus of Hungary. To secure his Italian possessions, he sought the backing of the anti-Venetian League of Upper Italy (Mantua and Milano were predominant) and in 1478 married Paola Gonzaga, the daughter of Ludovico III of Mantua.[71] His mother-in-law, Barbara von Hohenzollern used her many contacts to strengthen his interests in Görz. During many Imperial Council meetings, Leonhard sought backing against the Turks who had threatened his possessions since 1469 and the Emperor. Leonhard set great hopes in a closer connection with King Matthias Corvinus of Hungary, from whom he could have expected help against his primary enemy Emperor Frederick III, as well as against Venice, especially Hungarian forces in a war against the Emperor to not only take Vienna, but even to advance into Upper Carinthia and also wage war against the Venetians on the Dalmatian coast. For a long time, the Venetians had been active in the County of Görz, they constructed defensive works against the Turks on Görz territory, at the Isonzo Bridge at Farra, from which Gradisca developed. They did not worry in the slightest about protests from Görz and even to get Count Leonhard to sell his countship. They had already leased the important port of Latisana, a transfer point for inner-Austrian trade with Venice. The Venetians' continuing provocations gradually drove the counts back into the Habsburgs' arms. In 1487 rumors arose that the Count of Görz was seriously ill[72] and the county's succession could be expected in the foreseeable future, so the Signoria of Venice initiated secret negotiations with the Captain of Görz, Virgil von Graben. After the awaited death of the Count, he was to hand over the castle, city and county to the Republic of Venice, and in return receive all the Görz castles and lands in the Friuli region from Venice as fiefs, along with 20,000 ducats as payment. Virgil von Graben showed himself to not be averse to trading. However, the Count's health was not as poor as suspected.

---

69 Wiesflecker, Hermann, "Die Grafschaft Görz und die Herrschaft Lienz, ihre Entwicklung und ihr Erbfall an Österreich (1500)," in *Veröffentlichungen des Tiroler Landesmuseums Ferdinandeum*, 78/1998, (Innsbruck: Tiroler Landesmuseums Ferdinandeum, 1998), pp. 131–149, specifically p. 137.

70 A hereditary treaty was concluded with Sigismund of Tirol in 1463.

71 See Forcher, Michael, *Kleine Geschichte Tirols* (Innsbruck and Vienna: Haymon, 2012), p. 54.

72 On 29 March, the Archduke Sigismund wrote to Duke Albrecht IV of Bavaria-Munich that Count Leonhard was very ill. See Lichnowsky, Eduard Fürst von, *Geschichte des Hauses Habsburg. 8. Band (Kaiser Friedrich III. und sein Sohn Maximilian, 1477–1493)* (Vienna: Verlag Schaumburg und Compagnie, 1844), p. 624.

THE OUTBREAK OF HOSTILITIES

In March of 1487, the Archduke provoked the Venetian Republic with the confiscation of some (Venetian-run) mines in the Primiero and Sugana Valleys as well as by arresting 130 Venetian merchants and confiscating their wares at the Bolzano Fair on 23 April. The Venetian merchants were guaranteed safe passage to the Bolzano Fair by treaty, so their arrest was a blatant violation of the treaty. [73]

Sigismund sent a letter to the Emperor in which he complained about Venice. Furthermore, he had a letter handed over to the Doge in which all the Venetian alleged and actual misdeeds were listed. The letter was signed by 27 nobles, including the Ulrico and Andrea d'Arco brothers. Archduke Sigismund turned to the Swiss Confederation for assistance, which was flatly refused at the council meeting of Lucerne on 9 May 1487. But some of the cantons seemed to be cooperative, so Zurich and Zug allowed recruiting.

To finance the campaign, Sigismund deliberately did not rely on the Tirolean estates; he received 20,000 guilders [74] from the Bavarian dukes, and 13,000 from the banking houses of Paumgartner [75] and Fugger. Johann von Waldburg-Sonnenberg came up with the impressive sum of 12,000 guilders. However - and that was the point - the loan of 50,000 guilders was expected to be paid by the Bavarian dukes. And they were supposed to receive all of the Austrian Outlands as fiefs in return. For example, this was contained in a secret treaty from July 1487. [76]

Coat of arms of the von Matsch stewards (*Vögte*)

With the money (or a part of the money), it was possible to hire the best mercenaries in Europe: Swiss. Ulrich VII von Hohensax [77] entered Habsburg's service. He delivered a contingent of mercenaries from the Confederation to Tirolean Archduke Sigismund. [78] Conrad Gächuff brought additional mercenaries, primarily from Thurgau. [79] Mercenaries from Zurich came under the leadership of their

---

73 The Venetians reacted by moving their main transshipment point to Mittenwald, which belonged to the Bishopric of Freising at that time. Additionally, they drove off sheep herds from Tirolean subjects. See Knapton, Michael, *Venice and the Veneto during the Renaissance: the legacy of Benjamin Kohl*, (Florence: Firenze University Press, 2014), p. 227.

74 On 16 May 1487, Archduke Sigismund wrote to Duke Albrecht IV of Bavaria-Munic that he would repay the 4,000 guiders he had received in cash within a year.

75 The Augsburg line of this patrician family, which originated from Nuremberg, was active in Tirolean mining enterprises.

76 Sigismund's first written promises to Albrecht IV date from the year 1479.

---

77 Ulrich VII von Hohensax. 1463 to 1538, commander and diplomat. He was the son of Albrecht I von Hohensax, who died the year of Ulrich's birth, and the townswoman Ursula Mötteli. He was a citizen of Zurich.

78 The bulk of these forces consisted of free men from the Thurgau region. See Hürlimann, Louis, "Ulrich VII. von Hohensax (1463 - 1538), Gerichtsherr und Militärunternehmer" in *Thurgauer Beiträge zur Geschichte, Band 135* Frauenfeld: Historischer Verein des Kantons Thurgau, 1995), pp. 169–175, specifically: p. 170.

79 The spellings "Gäschuf", "Gegauf", "Gebuf" also existed. He was first mentioned in 1473 in Constance, also called "von Sigmundsee," he was a citizen of Kesswil. In 1474 he took part in the movement to Héricourt; in 1476 he was knighted before the Battle of Murten; and in 1477 he participated in the fighting in the Franche-Comté. Starting in 1480, he was in the service of Archduke Sigismund of Tirol, and in 1487 he led the Thurgau mercenaries in the Venetian War.

Swiss Mercenaries in the Upper Italian Wars in 1487

The year 1487 was especially abundant in operations over the Alps. That year the Swiss side carried out four wars in Italy, in which there was no lack of numerous volunteers.

At first the Bernese and the Freiburgers supported the Duke of Savoy in his feud with the Margrave of Saluzzo with a corps of 1,500 men. Besides these forces, he also received an influx of 1,200 men from the Oberland under the Count of Gruyere and a corps of volunteers (*Freischar*) under the captain Konrad Losner of Solothurn. The latter unit consisted of 300 Swiss fighters who had rushed there from the Low Countries where they had been in the service of the German King Maximilian. They distinguished themselves on many occasions, especially when the caused serious losses to a 4,000-man Piedmontite corps that was attempting to relieve the beleaguered town of Saluzzo. Alone, despite their courage their return to their homeland was forbidden: they were forced to spend their lives in exile because they had not complied with their Swiss authorities' prohibitions. In 1482, the Duke of Ferrara, Ercole I d´Este, in a feud with the Venetians, contracted a number of fighters from Canton Bern and other *Orte*, for example 300 from Appenzell and the Rhine Valley; the majority of them perished in a plague that broke out in the army. When, a few years later (1487), the Austrian Duke Sigismund, who was embroiled in a war with the Venetians over border disputes, recruited, using Bavarian money, a number of fighters from Zurich and Bern, from Thurgau and Graubunden, along with many Landsknecht from Swabia and the Lower Union (*Niiedrige Vereinigung*). These mercenaries, under Ulrich von Hohensax, distinguished themselves by their courageous behavior and provided the Duke good service, yet they were neglected and due to lack of payment left the Duke's army before the end of the war.

Another feud started between the regents of Milan and the free people in Hochrhätien because of curtailment of certain tax freedoms and other proprieties in which the latter were able to be victorious without foreign help. But it was indeed otherwise in the campaign which the Jost von Silenen, the Bishop of Wallis (Valais), undertook against Milan. When a four-year-long legal petition for old demands for old debts did not bear fruit, the Bishop was able to get the fellow countrymen of Wallis to take up arms in his behalf. With him went many bellicose youths from the Waldstätten under the leadership of two messengers from Schwyz and Unterwalden, who had been sent to the Bishop by the *Tagsatzung* in Zurich to hold off arming against Milan – which was not in the Confederations' mind – along with a patrol from Lucerne. Just from the careless conduct of the captains, the Wallisers and their allies suffered a loss of 800 men. The Swiss and France negotiated, the Wallisers got compensation; however, their hatred grew toward the Bishop, who they finally drove out of the country. The captains, through whose carelessness the defeat occurred and were also accused of cowardice, were brought home for severe punishment; the captain of the Lucerners, Hans Murer, was also thrown in jail for disobedience and an unauthorized feud and had his honor and possessions taken.

From: Rudolph, J. Martin, *Die Hülfs- und Freischaarenzüge der Schweizer seit der Gründung der Eidgenossenschaft bis zum Einfall in den Kanton Luzern im Mai 1845* (Zurich: Leuthy, 1846), p. 45. *Hochrhätien*, High Raetia, is the area around Chur in Grisons/Graubunden.

---

captain Lienhard Stämmli.[80] Sigismund's senior court administrator, Count Gaudenz von Matsch, was able to contribute hired men and some levies from the Graubünden (Grisons) and the Vinschgau, and in mid-April he was named the Archduke's most senior commander. There is more to say about this man and his illustrious family.

In the 15th century, the Matsches were one of the most important noble families in the Tirol-Graubunden region. The sparse ruins of the Obermatsch and Untermatsch castles lie in the Matsch Valley that were the main seats of the two separate lines of the family in the Vinschgau. In 1297 they were able to get possession of the Churburg (castle, also in the Vinschgau), which they expanded to be their main seat. The 'Stewards of Matsch" were servants and vassals of the Tirolean counts on one side and of the Bishop of Chur on the other side. Even when they attained the title of the "Counts," the designation of "Steward" ("*Vogt*", plural "*Vögte*") remained distinguishing. They had large land holdings in the Vinschgau and the Graubunden region. They even temporarily obtained the County of Kirchberg in Swabia through a marriage.

Count Gaudenz's year of birth cannot be determined, but one assumes it was probably 1436. His parents were Ulrich IX, Count (*Graf*) von Matsch[81] and his wife Agnes.[82] In descriptions, Gaudenz is shown as a completely jovial,

---

80 There was also a spelling as "Stamelin".

81 He was born in 1419 and giant in size. His impressive armor is in the armor room in the Churburg Castle. Ulrich von Matsch was Tirol's national commander (*Landeshauptmann*), that is the prince's deputy, starting in 1471

82 She came from the House of the Counts of Werdenberg-Sargans.

The Chur Castle (Churburg), Photo: Florian Messner

courteous and brave knight. Thanks to his upbringing at the court of Sigismund of Tirol, he had already traveled extensively in his youth, learned how to get around in high society, and took part in knightly mock combat. He began his political activities at the Castels Castle with the administration of the family property in the Prättigau region. Financial straits and the calculation of how to please the Archduke Sigismund caused Gaudenz to give up part of his property and only exercise control over it. By 5 March 1464, Ulrich von Matsch had sold the Tarasp Castle in the Lower Engadin (*Unterengadin*) to Sigismund the Rich-in-Coin for 2,000 guilders.[83] In 1470 Gaudenz made a pilgrimage to Jerusalem. Archduke Sigismund made him the Captain of the Etsch (Adige) and the Castle Count of the Tirol Castle on 30 June 1478.[84] His father, Ulrich, did not function in his official position from 1475 until his death in 1481. Until 1482, Gaudenz von Matsch moved about in Sigismund's service at the latter's court and on trips as a messenger. On 22 June 1482, Count Gaudenz had to resign from his post as Captain of the Etsch due to exceeding his authority. He had two men imprisoned and embarrassingly questioned (i.e., tortured) because he suspected a plot against the Archduke, but there was nothing there.[85] He went into the service of the Duke of Milan. Contact with him was already established by 1479 when he married Hippolyta, the daughter of the Milanese Chancellor Cicco Simonetta.[86] But starting in 1485 he was active again at Sigismund's court, in 1486 was named as the senior official at the Archduke's court (*erzherzoglichen Oberhofmeister*) and on 5 March 1487 was handed the stewardship of Feldkirch. Count Gaudenz was related to Count Jörg von Werdenberg-Sargans by marriage.[87] Both families had large properties in the Graubunden region, had close relations in the Swiss Confederation and were involved in many regional trade activities. What was

---

83 See Ladurner, P. Justinian, "Die Vögte von Matsch, später auch Grafen von Kirchberg" in *Zeitschrift des Ferdinandeums für Tirol und Vorarlberg*, Ser. 3, Bd. 18 (1873), p. 9.

84 For that he recieved an annual income of 900 guilders. See Ladurner, P. Justinian et al. (Eds.), *Archiv für Geschichte und Alterthumskunde Tirols*, Band 2 (Innsbruck: Wagner'sche Universitätsbuchhandlung, 1850), p. 34.

85 Jörg Häl von Maienburg became his successor. See Brandis, Jacob-Andrä, Freiherr von, *Die Geschichte der Landeshauptleute von Tirol* (Innsbruck: Wagner, 1850), p. 272.

86 No sons came from this marriage, only the daughter Catharina. Count Gaudenz still had three illegitimate daughters and an illegitimate son.

87 Jörg von Werdenberg-Sargans was the Guardian (*Pfleger*) of Landeck starting in 1485.

decisive was that Gaudenz von Matsch and Jörg von Werdenberg-Sargans along with Count Oswald Thierstein belonged to the trio of influential courtiers around whom a band of influential counselors grouped at the Innsbruck court, the so-called "bad counselors" ("*bösen Räte*").[88] Oswald von Thierstein had held high command positions in the Burgundian Wars. But his role was controversial.[89] But there were other veterans of the Burgundian Wars who were considered competent.

Just as willingly as the nobles of the Outlands (*Vorland*) had taken up arms against the Swiss Confederation, did they stream now to arms. The Duke got strong support from the Outlands.

For example, Smassmann II von Rappoltstein[90] rushed with 62 horses and men-at-arms (*Reisigen*) via Reutte to Tirol, as did Philipp and Simon von Pfirt (Ferrette), Hans Walch von Ranspach, Christoph and Heinrich von Hattstatt, Ludwig and Jacob von Maasmünster and many others who went the same way. However, among the first was Friedrich Kappler, whose cavalry ("*geraissig zeug*"), including wagon horses that "transported powder" ("*pulffer fuerten*"),[91] was already in Tirol in April.[92] He probably had the task of gathering the arrivals in Innsbruck. At the end of May the foot soldiers, about 1,000 men-at-arms arrived there from the County of Hauenstein and the Sundgau and Breisgau regions.[93] Around this time, Kappler crossed the Brenner Pass and on 2 June was already in Klausen as "field commander of a small corps." In his personal retinue there was a scribe, Hans von Esslingen, and a doctor, Ch. Thierberg, as well as a trumpeter. "Nikolo and Hanns the Stariots", Konrad von Kempten and Walther von Andlau[94] appear to have been recruited by him. Also Wilhelm Kappler was among them, as well as Peter Kappler, but who was not part of the family. A man from Basel, Claus Murer from a patrician family joined them.[95] A Bavarian contingent (from the Duchy of Bavaria-Munich) joined the Tirolean Archduke's army: a no further determinable number of men led by Alexander

Coat of arms of the Counts of Thierstein
(from the *Scheiblerschen Wappenbuch*)

---

88 Gaudenz von Matsch belonged to the supporters of an alliance with the Dukes of Wittesbach.

89 For his services, Emperor Friedrich III awarded Count Oswald von Thierstein with the Hohkönigsburg (Castle) in the Alsace in 1479: on 14 May 1479 an imperial order was given to the city of Strasbourg to help the Thiersteins take possession of the (destroyed) Hohkönigsburg. In doing this, the Emperor wanted to prevent the Kurpfalz's increase of power in the Alsace. Oswald and his brother had to deeply indebt themselves – a total of 11,000 guilders - to the cities of Strasbourg and Solothurn in order to undertake their ambitious construction on the Hohkönigsburg. Graf Oswald was in fierce arguments with the City of Basel in 1481 and 1482 about this. The contentious issue was primarily about the rules for the cloister at the Klingenthal nunnery. In this way, the Count von Thierstein got the derisive nickname of the "Consoler of Nuns" ("*Nonnentröster*").

90 Smaßmann, born in 1437, had been a treasurer for Charles the Bold. In 1483 he traveled in the company of Caspar Zorn von Bulach and the Kurmainz treasurer deacon Bernhard von Breitenbach to Jerusalem and to the Catharine Monastery in the Sinai. In Jerusalem he was made a Knight of the Holy Sepulcher. In 1484 he returned, and in 1499 he had a small chapel built in memory of the pilgrimage. He died in 1517.

91 They apparently pulled the wagons loaded with gunpowder barrels.

92 Kappler, who had proven himself many times in the Burgundian Wars, appeared as the "Field Commander of the Cavalry of the Outland" ("*Feldhauptmann des Geraisigen Zeugs der vordern Lannd*"). See Hormayr, Joseph von, *Taschenbuch für vaterländische Geschichte*, Band 8 (Leipzig: Georg Franz, 1837), p. 343.

93 A large part, if not all of them, were commanded by the knight (*Ritter*) Dietrich von Blumegg.

94 While one can clearly identify the just named men as coming from the Allgäu and the Lower Alsace, the meaning of the term "*Stariotten*" in the sources is unclear. It could have been meant as "*Stradioten*," light cavalry from the Balkans.

95 According to so-called "*Dienstrevers*" (service agreement) with Archduke Sigismund, he was paid with two horses, that is, one for himself and one for his page. A knight or a gentleman always rode with at least two mounts ("*zweispännig*").

Heavily armored Tirolean soldiers
Photo: Condottieri Mauriziani

Donning armor was a lengthy affair and hardly possible by oneself, especially for the shoulders and arms.
Photo: Città del Grifo

von Pappenheim and Hans Pienzenauer. Hans von Freiberg, Hans von Hirschberg and Ludwig von Rechberg also belonged among them. [96]

Duke Sigismund demanded neither money nor fighters from the Tirolean estates. Thus initially there were hardly any Tiroleans were in the ranks of the Duke's army, except for the ducal vassals in Tirol and ducal officials. [97] The levy from the area under the Landeck jurisdiction was a prominent exception. [98] The Prince's serfs were also levied, although not very many of them. [99]

Georg Gossembrot, one of the most valued financial experts of his time, was responsible for supplying the army. He acquired oats and grain for the levies from the Outlands that moved via the Arlberg to Landeck. He purchased rye and oats – in 1487 quite cheaply – in Bavaria (in the Ries, in Dillingen, in Augsburg, Kaufbeuren and Füssen). The money was loaned in part by the Duke Georg of Bayern-Landshut. The supplies were brought over the Brenner, Finstermünz and Reschen Passes to Bolzano.

---

96 See Würdinger, Joseph, *Kriegsgeschichte von Bayern, Franken, Pfalz und Schwaben von 1347 bis 1506*, Band 2 (Munich: Cotta'sche Buchhandlung, 1868), p. 145.

97 For example, Count Graf Wilhelm von Werdenberg-Sargans, a brother of Count Jörg, was among the participants on the campaign. See. Hegi, Friedrich, *Die geächteten Räte des Erzherzogs Sigmund von Österreich und ihre Beziehungen zur Schweiz, 1487 - 1499: Beiträge zur Geschichte der Lostrennung der Schweiz vom Deutschen Reiche* (Innsbruck: Wagner'sche Universitätsbuchhandlung, 1910), p. 9.

98 This exception can perhaps be explained in that the archducal steward of Landeck, Count Jörg von Werdenberg-Sargans, belonged to the influential group of counselors who pushed for a war with Venice.

99 They were the "*Eigenleute*" from Imst, who were the serfs of the Starkenberg family and went over into princely ownership after the Starkenbergs were driven out.

ROVERETO

The town and castle of Rovereto were held by strong Venetian forces under Nicolo de Priuli. The overall command of the Venetian forces in the theater was carried out by Giulio Cesare da Varano.[100]

Matsch decided to attack the town before strong Venetian forces could be assembled. Therefore, he moved with his 8,000 to 10,000-man army before the town and had it fired upon heavily. However, Priuli, with his defenders reinforced by the town's citizens, was able to repulse the first assault. With all haste, the Venetians gathered their forces in Lombardy and around Lake Garda and called upon the population to fight. A relief army for Rovereto was to be formed. The Tiroleans set up a field camp in front of the town and began a formal siege. On 13 May, Gaudenz von Matsch wrote from the camp at Rovereto, in the name of Archduke Sigismund, to Bishop Ortlieb[101] of Chur, telling him to order the members of his bishopric in the Vinschgau to sell the Steward of Mals oxen and other necessary supplies to the army," a lot of money" ("*vmbain zimlich gelt*") because it was essential.[102]

During the siege of Rovereto "bombs" fired into the town were described in older accounts as "thin iron balls filled with tar pitch".[103] This barrage caused extensive damage and a great panic.[104] Priuli, the Venetian commander of the town, was able with the help of a certain "Thomas del Murer of Brentoniko", to bring munitions and men into the town. A breach in the wall and repeated Tirolean assaults forced Priuli to withdraw with his men into the castle.[105] That was on 30 May 1487.[106] Some Tirolean levies are said to have distinguished themselves during the attacks.

For the troops from the Landeck jurisdiction, there is even still a written commendation by Gaudenz von Matsch for their actions:

"Count Gaudenz von Matsch, Senior Field Command to the wise, honorable and common inhabitants of the Landeck court district. After you, in order to please my graceful lord, employed a number of infantrymen at Rovereto, who were gone longer than you had thought, these people suffered injuries, but it was only for your and our lord's benefit.

Your people were obedient, diligent and honest, so I want to praise and help them and you with my most gracious lord, in order to compensate for your damages. Written in Rovereto on the evening of St. Margaret's Day, in the year 1487."[107]

In some chronicles, there is even talk that Count Gaudenz had acted hesitantly, yes, even indecisively and that his subordinates had to take matters into their own hands.[108]

On the Venetian side, there was then a change in command. The previous commander, Giulio Cesare da Varano, was actually the second choice. His predecessor as commander of the Venetian armed forces was the famous Condottiere Count Roberto da Sanseverino d´Aragona. However, he had (temporarily) departed with his staff and troops to his old home Naples where he fought in the "Barons' War" from 1485 to 1486. In 1486 he returned to his base Cittadella, but without being given back his old command.[109] In Venice, after the Tirolean's first successes, it was deemed necessary to call him back and entrust him with command of a large army.

---

100 He was born in 1430 as the son of the lord of Camerino. He became the successor of his father, Giovanni in 1444. He served the popes as a commander: initially starting in 1429 for Pope Paul II and later for Pope Sixtus IV. In 1482 he entered the service of the Kingdom of Aragon. In the conflicts between the popes and the Venetian Republic in the 1490s, he became the Republic's General Commandant. In 1502 he was murdered at the orders of Cesare Borgia. In the older descriptions, he appears as "Camerin" or "Camerino".

101 Ortlieb von Brandis was born in 1430 in the Brandis Castle (in Graubünden), he became the Bishop of Chur in 1458 and died on 25 July 1491.

102 See Lichnowsky, *Geschichte des Hauses Habsburg*, p. 626.

103 "[D]ünne eiſernen Kugeln mit Pech gefüllt," *Allgemeiner National-Kalender für Tirol und Vorarlberg*, Band 5 (Innsbruck: Wagner´sche Universitätsbuchhandlung 1825), p. 3.

104 It is unclear how these projectiles were fired. Whether they were mortar rounds fired from gunpowder cannon is at least questionable. It could have been a kind of "Greek fire" shot from a trebuchet or similar catapult. In the Weissenburg Bishops' War ("*Weißenburger Stiftsfehde*"), Electoral Prince Frederick of the Platinate used such catapults in the winter of 1469-70 at the siege of Weissenburg. But they were positioned to far from the town to cause any damage, which possibly could have even been planned by the Electoral Prince. See Seehase u. Ollesch, *Kurfürst Friedrich der Siegreiche von der Pfalz (1425-1476)* (Petersberg: Imhof, 2012), p. 66.

105 Ibid., p. 3.

106 In a letter, dated only one day later, from the Doge of Venice to Emperor Frederick III, the Venetian head of state declared that Venice was forced to go to war with the Archduke Sigismund.

107 "*Grave Gaudenz von Metsch Obrister Veldhaubtmann an die weysen, erbarn und beschaiden gemainen gerichtsleut des gerichtes L a n n d e g k meinen gueten gunnern. - Mein willig dinst zuvor. Nachdem ir meinem gnedigisten herren zue gevallen ain anzal fueßvolck in seiner gnaden ve l d vor R o v e r e i d gehalten, dieselben villaicht lenger ausbleiben, dann ir vermaint hättet und deshalben schaden geliten und genomen, daz alles meinem gnedigisten herrn und euch zue guet beschehen. Nu haben sich die euren willig, vleißig und redlich gehalten, des ich euch und sy bey meinem gnedigisten herren beruemen und auch eure schaden zu widerlegen beholfen sein. Geben zu Rovereid an sand Margareten abend anno 1487.*" From Gstraunthaler, Olt. Dr. Gerhard, *Die Schlacht bei Calliano am 10. August 1487, Zur Geschichte des Laudegg-Fähnleins von 1496*, at www.tiroler-schuetzen.at.

108 Naturally that could also have been an embellishment in light of the Tirolean commander's later actions.

109 See Mallet, M.E. and Hale, J.R., *The Military Organisation of Renaissance State: Venice c.1400 to 1617* (Cambridge: Cambridge University Press, 1984), p. 53.

The armor of this Venetian captain with its asymmetrical shoulder pieces and the meshwork on his leg armor is typically Italian.
Also the *giornea*, an often expensive, sleeveless, outer garment, open at the sides, that was gathered in many folds with a waistbelt, is characteristic of Italian fashion of the 15th century. It was worn over civilian clothing as well as over the armor in war.
Photo: Città del Grifo

Rovereto Castle - its appearance today differs starkly from 1487 due to later renovations.
Photo: Florian Messner

Rovereto Castle, Photo: Florian Messner

A troop of Tirolean horsemen at a break
The men dismount and are attended by baggage train personnel. They wear both Italian and northern Alpine style armor. Italian armor has a compact shape and is characterized by large blank surfaces, projecting shoulder-pieces and large elbow cops. Their northern Alpine counterparts are clearly more gracefully built and have surfaces with ridges and clusters of folds.
Photo: Christopher Retsch

THE DUEL

Condottiere Count Roberto da Sanseverino d´Aragona was already somewhat greyed from the burdens of his age, and he took his son Antonio Maria with him on the campaign. This third oldest son of the old commander was born in 1460 or 1461 and appears in documents for the first time in 1481 on the occasion of a wild boar hunt with this brother Gaspare. Other than that, he was present at the siege of Ficarolo. While his father was besieging the town, Antonio Maria (again together with his brother Gaspare) captured the Canda and Castelguglielmo Bastions and the Tower of San Donato. When his father became seriously ill in 1482, Antonio Maria temporarily took over the command. On 7 May 1486 he played a decisive role in the Battle of Montorio. But he was also famous as a tournament combatant. In February of 1485, he and his brothers Gaspare and Galezzzo took part in a great tournament. Antonio and Gaspare took the first prize: 25 gold ducats and precious cloth worth twelve ducats. Galeazzo, who was considered one of Italy's best horsemen and tournament combatants also won a prize.[110] The knightly duel still remained part of the ideals of a young nobleman, on both the Italian and Tirolean sides.

Because both armies had set up their camps on the respective banks of the Adige, not far from one another, it offered the opportunity for a dramatic Intermezzo.[111]

Thereupon, on 7 June, Antonio Maria da Sanseverino sent a trumpeter with a challenge to the assembled German nobles in the Tirolean camp, that one should name a combatant with whom he could measure up with in the knightly fashion of the ancient heroes. The answer came promptly. The young Johann von Waldburg-Sonnenberg[112] wanted to fight and had already obtained the permission from his commander, Count Gaudenz von Matsch. Because the two combatants did not serve the same lord, hostages had to be exchanged who guaranteed with their lives (in reality with ransoms) that each combatant would appear at the established time and place. The site (across the Adige below the Pradaglia Castle ruins) for the duel was set.[113] In doing so, those overseeing the duel took care that neither combatant would be disadvantaged by the position of the sun. The prize for the duel was set: the winner should receive 1,000 ducats as well as the loser's horse and armor. A lance, sword, dagger and mace were permitted as weapons.[114]

There was also a kind of life insurance. The winner, should he kill his opponent, would only receive the horse and armor, but not the 1,000 ducats. A signal for yielding was established so there would be no misunderstandings. The password was to be "Santa Catharina". There were important regulations for the spectators. For example, so that neither combatant would be disadvantaged by shouts, gestures and so forth, such acts were punishable by threat of death. Only the seconds and judges ("*Grieswarte*"), of which each opponent was allowed four to accompany himself, were permitted to speak to the combatant. In one of the descriptions of the duel, it said that gallows had been set up near the dueling site to ensure the spectators followed the rules.

Antonio Maria da Sanseverino was already considered an exceptionally gifted tournament knight in his younger years.

Old engraving in the author's archives

---

110 Galeazzo later succeeded not only as a Condottiere, but also as a patron of the arts and an art collector. He was a close friend of Leonardo da Vinci.

111 There are various descriptions of the duel and the circumstances about those accompanying in contemporary or relatively contemporary chronicles. The closest in time was the chronicle by Konrad Wenger which originated before the end of the 15th century. A few decades newer were the depictions by the Venetians Marco Antonio Coccio and the Cardinal Pietro Bembo.

112 How young he was is difficult to establish. Different years for his birth are given in the chronicles: from 1437 to 1458 and 1460 to 1470.

113 For that reason, the duel is called the "*Disfida di Pardaglia*" in Italian.

114 A very detailed and worth reading account of the duel is at talhoffer.wordpress.com.

This illustration from the "Stewards' Chronicles" shows Johann von Waldburg-Sonnenberg.
Pappenheim´sche Truchsessenchronik

On the day of the combat, 12 June 1487, the duelists initially went against one another in a knightly joust, so a barrier had been erected. Waldburg missed his opponent with his lance, but the other was able to score a blow to Waldburg's chest. In doing so, Sanseverino's lance shattered and a piece hit his horse that bolted in surprise. It ran right into the barrier and Sanseverino fell from his saddle. He stood up and approached his opponent. Waldburg, still mounted, attacked him, but his mount shied. Then Sanseverino pounced at him and took his long sword.[115] Waldburg turned his horse around and fled, then jumped out of the saddle. With a dagger in one hand and a mace in the other, he went straight at his opponent. Suddenly he threw down the mace, which his Tirolean spectators - , flabbergasted and appalled - took as a sign that he was yielding. But Waldburg had not thought to give up. Meanwhile, Sanseverino realized that he now had both his own as well as the German's sword. He kept Waldburg's sword and ran at Waldburg. With all his might, he struck at him with the sword, but its previous owner turned to the side. The sword blow went through thin air and Waldburg attacked his opponent. Both wrestled, Sanseverino tried to throw his opponent over his hip but was unsuccessful. Both fell to the ground. Waldburg's head was under Sanseverino's right arm, but his right leg was on top of the Italian's body. Waldburg was able with his left hand to grasp the dagger, which he held in his right hand, whereby he cut his hand. He was, however, able to shove the dagger under Sanseverino's armor skirting and stab him multiple times. Then Sanseverino cried out the password "Santa Catharina" to signal his giving up. Waldburg fell to his knees and thanked his creator.

More important than the outcome of the fight was the fact that on the previous day, i.e., on 11 June, the Rovereto Castle had fallen into the Tiroleans' hands.[116]

Priuli had bravely held out, but realized that given the damages, his lack of provisions and the Tiroleans repeated attacks, there was no more hope to wait for relief to arrive. He surrendered the castle to Gaudenz von Matsch. The garrison fled to Mori via the bridge at Ravazzone.

In the meantime, Swiss mercenaries had reached the Tirolean arm, to which the Venetians had just sent their letter of refusal. When the Zurichers arrived at the Tirolean Army's camp on 13 June, they found 800 other Swiss already there. The Zurich contingent itself included 350 Zurichers and 40 other Swiss.[117] Between the Swiss and the other members of the Tirolean Army, especially the Blumegg foot soldiers, there appears to have been friction.[118]

---

115 Supposedly it was an armor-piercing sword (*Bohrschwert*), a so-called "*Bratspieß*" (scewer).

116 See Welber, Mariano, *La battaglia di Calliano 10 agosto 1487. Cronaca desunta dalle fonti narrative* (Calliano: Comune di Calliano, 1987), pp. 44–57.

117 See Nell, Martin, *Die Landsknechte, Entstehung der ersten deutschen Infanterie* (Berlin: Eberling, 1914), p. 198.

118 See Rudolph, J. Martin, *Kriegsgeschichte der Schweizer seit Gründung des Schweizerbundes bis zum ewigen Frieden mit Frankreich* (Baden: Zehnder´sche Buchhandlung, 1847), p. 227.

Armor-piercing sword
(*Bohrschwert*) and sheath
Photo: Stefan Roth

Thrusting dagger
(*Scheibendolch*),
grip arrangement
Photo: Stefan Roth

Thrusting dagger's hilt
(*Scheibendolch*)
Photo: Stefan Roth

Castel Pietra (lower right) and Castel Beseno (in background), Photo: Florian Messner

GAUDENZ VON MATSCH WITHDRAWS

At the end of June provisioning problems were visibly noticeable for the Tiroleans. Gaudenz von Matsch tried to intercept and capture the Venetian supplies that were coming from the direction of Lake Garda. For this purpose, he had positioned a contingent of about 800 men on road on the right side of the Adige that led to Nago. After the last negotiations with the Venetians fell apart, a meeting engagement took place on 3 July 1487[119] with Sanseverino's forces at Ravazzone that ended with neither victors nor vanquished, during which Roberto Sanseverino's son Antonio Maria was captured. Allegedly he had rushed to aid his father, who had been pushed back into the Adige in the close combat. Roberto Sanseverino barely escaped drowning or capture, but his son Antonio Maria fell into the enemy's hands. Shortly thereafter, surprisingly the Tirolean commander completely withdrew toward Innsbruck, without stopping in Trento and only leaving a small rearguard in Rovereto.[120] However, he did not destroy the bridge over the Adige at Rovereto.[121] A Venetian advance through the Sugana Valley (*Valsugana*) would have been an explanation that would have cut off the Tirolean Army's retreat route. In any case, Matsch completely quit the region. Did he suspect an attack in the west that would have also been aimed at his own possessions? It is not very likely, but still possible that he was concerned about an upheaval in Innsbruck and wanted to rapidly pre-empt threatening developments

---

119 According to other accounts, it was on 4 July 1487.

120 Not agreeing with this, another account states that Gaudenz von Matsch could have covered his retreat on 7 July 1487 by setting the Rovereto Castle on fire. See Gober, Manuel, *Museo Storico Italiano della Guerra Rovereto* (Rovereto, 2008), pp. 38–40.

121 See Daublebsky von Sterneck, Moritz Ritter, *Geschichtlicher Anhang zur militärischen Beschreibung des Kriegsschauplatzes Tirol und Vorarlberg* (Vienna: Gerold, 1872), p. 16.

there. On 18 May, King Maximilian[122] had named Gaudenz von Matsch as the Senior Captain and Governor of Tirol and the Outlands in the case of Sigismund's death. He also would have received the *Kastvogtei*[123] authority over the Bishoprics of Brixen and Trento. It is possible that this development, which Gaudenz could have first learned of a few days later, could have influenced his decision.[124] In any case, the sudden retreat undermined his political position. In many accounts, there is talk of treason and of Venetian bribery. In any case, Gaudenz von Matsch was in contact with Venice's political leaders through emissaries, but it is unclear whether he acted at the orders or intent of Archduke Sigismund. Perhaps it was not at all the Count departing with the army, but rather the army with the Count. The Swiss mercenaries were not paid in accordance with their contract, in any case a large por-

---

122 On 16 February 1486, Maximilian, at his father's instigation, was elected the Roman-German King in the Imperial Cathedral (*Kaiserdom*) in Frankfurt am Main. Two months later, on 9 April 1486 his coronation took place in the Imperial Cathedral in Aachen.

123 "Kastvogtei (or *Schirmvogtei* or *Kastenvogtei*) is a legal term of Alemannic origin that was valid from the High Middle Ages into the early modern period. When taking on the office of the *Kastvogtei* or *Schirmvogtei*, feudal lords became responsible for the protective oversight of a monastery or bishopric and for certain tasks in the monastic commercial management (*Kasten* = granary), its jurisdiction and the legal representation externally and before the courts. In return, the *Kastvogt* or *Schirmvogt* received a part of the tithes.

124 Maximilian had the corresponding document issued in Flemish Bruges. See Lichnowsky, *Geschichte des Hauses Habsburg*, p. 627.

A group of horsemen in front of a field encampment. Photo: Christopher Retsch

tion of the army did not receive their payment.[125] It is possible that Gaudenz von Matsch had to disband the army because of a shortage of provisions and money.[126]

Reinforcements from the Churwalden region that belonged to the Ten Court Union (*Zehngerichtebund* – in Graubunden) were sent home in the middle of their march because there was no money to pay them.[127]

In Trento, Friedrich Kappler was in command (he had left for Trento on 20 July). The garrison consisted of 300 horsemen and some foot soldiers.

In the Giudicarie[128] (German: *Judikarien*) region, Parisotto de Lodron, as an ally of Venice, advanced to the north; on Lake Garda the Venetian garrison of Riva besieged the Tenno Castle. However, the defenders, led by the Count of Arco, were able to foil all the Venetian attempts to capture the castle.

About this time – if not before then – a Venetian noblewoman, named Mattea Collalto, informed her relative Odorico d'Arco about the content of the messages that

---

125 This is the talk in the older descriptions, see Rudolph, J. Martin, *Die Hülfs- und Freischaarenzüge der Schweizer seit der Gründung der Eidgenossenschaft bis zum Einfall in den Kanton Luzern im Mai 1845* (Zurich: Leuthy, 1846), p. 45.

126 See Hegi, *Die geächteten Räte des Erzherzogs Sigmund von Österreich*, p. 86.

127 "Besides, the Landtag of Meran, for poorly considered frugality, had those going from Churwalden and the Rhine turn around." ("*Zudem ließ der Landtag zu Meran, aus übelberechneter Sparsamkeit, neue Zuzüger aus Churwalden und am Rhein wieder umkehren.*") in Rudolph, *Kriegsgeschichte der Schweizer*, p. 227.

128 Giudicarie (German: *Judikarien*) is the designation of the region northwest of Lake Garda.

were exchanged between Venice and Sanseverino. Her brother, Giambattista Collalto[129] was definitely an accessory to this treasonous act.

Sanseverino advanced only very slowly, he could not clearly explain Gaudenz von Matsch's hasty retreat and suspected a trap. That would refute the thesis that Match committed treason. Sanseverino recaptured Rovereto on 25 July. The Nomi Castle was also captured quickly by his forces, but the Pietra Castle held out. Sanseverino wanted the castle taken quickly therefore, the commander positioned the bulk of his forces on the north side of the castle where it was easiest to attack, while two smaller detachments occupied the right and left banks of the Adige River at Nomi and Volano and remained in contact via a bridge composed of boats. On 31 July, the city of Hall sent twenty hand-gunners, and on 2 August, another thirty-four to Trento.[130] The beginning of August, the Venetians attacked and scattered a levy of peasants. In the meantime, reinforcements from the Outlands and Graubunden arrived in Trento. Mountain residents who were fleeing brought news of the Venetians' advance toward Trento, where Friedrich Kappler commanded as the City Captain.[131]

Gaudenz von Matsch

Meanwhile, the senior commander, Steward Gaudenz von Matsch moved with the assembled ducal army, 8,000-10,000 men, forcefully to Trento and decided immediately to take the Venetian town of Rovereto before the Venetians could put an orderly army in the field. On St. George's Day he arrived in front of the town with his troops and a great number of heavy cannon and when his demand to surrender was rejected by the Venetian garrison, he began to fiercely bombard the town, plundered and destroyed the houses outside the town, and made an assault, which, however the Venetian city commander, Nicolo de Priuli and the Venetian garrison was able to repel with the help of the citizens, whereupon Gaudenz von Matsch withdrew and laid waste to the surrounding area. – With the unsuccessful attempt on Rovereto and the growing number of forces at Serravalle, He did not in the least let the encamped Venetians made the mistake; they attacked the camp outside the town and began a proper siege. After several days, he bombarded the city walls with heavy cannons and attempted to knock them down - a kind of bombing that especially caused the garrison a great embarrassment. Finally, by shooting breaches in the walls and repeated assaults, von Matsch forced the Venetian praetor Priuli to surrender the town in the last days of May. – The latter had withdrawn with the remainder of his men into the castle, but because its defensive works had already suffered so much from the Tirolean's projectiles, and because there was so little hope of relief, a few days later he surrendered himself and his men at their mercy. – On 30 May Steward Gaudenz was master of the town and the castle of Rovereto. The Venetians, startled by capture of the town and Rovereto Castle, were enraged about the inaction of their former commander Giulio di Camarin, dismissed him, and in his place sent Roberto de San Severino, one of the greatest warriors of his time, as the commander into Tirol.

From: Ladurner, P. Justinian, "Die Vögte von Matsch, später auch Grafen von Kirchberg" in: *Zeitschrift des Ferdinandeums für Tirol und Vorarlberg*, Ser. 3, Bd. 18 (Innsbruck: Tiroler Landesmuseum Ferdinandeum, 1873) pp. 5-159, here: pp. 101–102.

---

129 The Captain of Trento was made aware of this very important information.

130 See Nell, *Die Landsknechte*, p. 211.

131 Additionally there was still a garrison in the Telvana Castle under Dietrich von Blumegg.

Castel Pietra, Photo: Florian Messner

THE BATTLE OF CALLIANO

In the Giudicarie things were changing slowly. The Lodron's levies now stood opposed to the soldiers under field commander Nikolas Firmian[132] and commander Micheletto Segato.[133] He had 400 Tirolean "youths" ("*Knappen*") under his command. The local Giudicarian levy was added to that. The fighting there ended with the capture of Paris Otto, who was brought to Innsbruck. The Bishop of Trento's troops, who were positioned on the Durone Pass and at Lake Garda, were then called to Trento. Segato followed with his people.

It remained for Kappler to gather the scattered detachment and to lead them against the Venetians. Literally at the last minute, he received reinforcements from the Tirolean militia *(Landsturm)*.

It was Friday, 10 August 1487. The local militia (around 400 men) and the Trento burghers (around 600 of them) under Georg von Ebenstein, advanced over the heights at Calliano to the south. Kappler advanced with 1,000 men (including the cavalry) on the country road from Trento against the Venetians. They occupied an unfavorable position between the Pietra Castle and the Adige River, so that they have little room to maneuver. The battle began at 1 o'clock in the afternoon. The day was unusually hot. There was an overhasty attack by the Tirolean vanguard under Micheletto Segato that had little effect but led to the loss of 200 men. Then Kappler attacked with his core troops – from Alsace, Breisgau, Basel and some from Tirol.[134] He employed most of his foot soldiers as pikemen, as in the Swiss fashion. But the Venetian ranks still held. Their infantry withdrew slowly back to the bridge of boats, but the cavalry, 1,200 horsemen under Sanseverino's personal leadership and his deputy Guido de Rossi, held the Tiroleans in check. Kappler's 200 horsemen could do little about it. Then the Landsturm and those from Trento under Georg von Ebenstein joined the fighting and struck the Venetians in the right flank.[135] About 18:00, the Venetians gave ground. Their cavalry pushed their own infantry up against the boat-bridge. The commander, Count Roberto da Sanseverino d'Aragona, tried in vain to bring order to his troops' movements. The soldiers pushed en masse onto the boat-bridge which collapsed under the weight.[136] Hundreds drowned in the Adige, among them Count Roberto. After Sanseverino's death, Guido de' Rossi took over command of the Venetian forces and attacked the Tiroleans with his 300 heavy cavalrymen, among them his son Filippo Maria, and 300 mounted archers. The Tiroleans suffered casualties from this relief attack, but not especially significant ones. Thanks to Kappler's superior field commander's skill, the Habsburg forces only had

---

132 He was the hereditary marshal of Trento starting in 1478.

133 In some older accounts, he appears as "Michelat Segato".

134 There were not more, especially many Swiss with the Tirolean army, but Valerius Anshelm states in his chronicle that the Swiss had fought at Calliano. See Anshelm, Valerius, Berner Chronik, Erster Band (1st Vol.) (Bern: L.A. Haller, 1825, p. 390.

135 See Nell, *Die Landsknechte*, p. 216.

136 Some chroniclers spoke of Kappler having had the boat-bridge attacked, which is not unlikely, he would only have had to have tree trunks or something similar send down the Adige.

Battlefield at Calliano, Photo Florian Messner

to regret minor losses - of around 500 men. His actions clearly showed the Swiss school of warfare: During the Burgundian Wars, they had on many occasions divided their army into several divisions but had them attack in agreed attack columns (like in the Battle of Nancy).

In the evening of the battle, Kappler left the battlefield to spend the night in Trento and returned the following morning. Sanseverino's body was found in a swampy part of the riverbank below the Pietra Castle. It was taken to Trento where it was buried with all honors.[137]

Then Kappler pleaded to march directly against Venice and the Venetians began to hastily recruit new cavalrymen and pull back toward Trento. In response, the Republic 'again recruited foreigners[138] and continued the war by attacks into Tirolean territory, but always without success. The Tiroleans supposedly conducted six successful defensive actions.

On 14 August 1487, four days after the Battle of Calliano, Kaiser Frederick III, who was in Nuremberg, answered the Doge Agostino Barbarigo.

The Kaiser blamed his cousin, the Archduke, for having begun the war against his wishes. Maximillian, the Roman King and son of Frederick III also distanced himself from Sigismund's starting the war.

At the *Landtag* in Hall on 16 August 1487, Archduke Sigismund dismissed his former counselors under pressure from the Tirolean estates. The chronically bankrupt Sigismund had always entertained plans to lease parts of this domains to raise money.[139] It came to an intervention on the part of the Kaiser when Archduke Sigismund carried out his accustomed leasing, this time to Duke Albrecht of Bavaria-Munich.[140] If all of the arrangements had achieved the force of law, and if Duke Albrecht, after

---

137 Sanseverino's remains were later taken to Milano where they were interred in the Church of San Francesco.

138 Five thousand new horsemen were recruited, but never employed. See Mallett and Hale, *The Military Organisation of Renaissance State*, p. 54.

139 Archduke Sigismund's first debentures to Duke Albrecht dated from the year 1479.

140 Albrecht IV of Bavaria- Munich (Bayern-München) exploited his friend Sigismund's weak will and lack of money, in that in July of 1487 he arranged a secret treaty that he should get all of outer Austria for the tiny sum of 50,000 guilders.

the demise of the old and increasingly more senile-acting Archduke Sigismund, had become the heir to Tirol and the Outlands, it would not only have had unpredictable consequences for the Habsburgs but also for the politics of the Empire. At the *Landtag* – in the presence of Imperial and Swiss Confederation representatives – a provisional government was created, in which representatives of the Outlands were prominently represented: Count Albrecht von Sulz, Kaspar von Mörsberg, Heinrich von Rechberg.[141] Along with fourteen Tiroleans, the government, under Chancellor Conrad Stürtzel, included eight men from the Outlands and two Imperial counselors.[142]

On 27 August, King Maximilian offered to be the mediator between Tirol and Venice. He and his father, who was mostly busy with the campaign against Hungary, was outspokenly displeased about the war between Tirol and Venice. On 12 October 1487, the Doge of Venice sent a very conciliatory letter to Archduke Sigismund. He empowered emissaries on 15 October for peace talks with Venice. Some of those emissaries are known by name: Benedikt Fueger (Dean of the Brixen Cathedral), *Ritter* (knight) Siegmund von Welsperg, *Ritter* Christoph von Hattstatt, *Ritter* Nikolaus von Firmian, Walter von Stadion, Matthäus Getzner (Mayor of Hall), Sigmund Gerstel (Mayor of Bolzano), Jost Alpershofer (Steward of the Strassberg Castle) and Martin Strauss.[143]

Through mediation by the Count of Arco, a peace treaty was concluded on 13 November 1487 between Venice and Tirol that essentially restored the status quo ante. In the treaty, it was agreed that all the villages that the Counts of Lodron had captured during the war would be returned to the Prince-Bishop of Trento and the Storo fortresses would be razed. However, the formal transfer of jurisdiction only occurred the following year and went to Pankratz Kühn, the Captain of Trento and emissary of the Archduke of Tirol.

Friedrich Kappler seemed to be unsatisfied with the results. A contemporary who knew him expressed the following: "Had Duke Sigismund committed with the Sundgauers and the Breisgauers, like Lord Friedrich Gappler (sic, Kappler) desired, then Venice could have been won, when Venice was ready to flee."[144]

Sanseverino's grave slab, Photo: Florian Messner

---

141 The new counselors additionally included: Benedikt Füeger, Degen Fuchs, Nikolaus von Firmian, Paul von Lichtenstein, Thomas von Freundsberg, Walter von Stadion and Heinrich Anich. See Köfler, Werner, *Land, Landschaft, Landtag: Geschichte der Tiroler Landtage von den Anfängen bis zur Aufhebung der Landständischen Verfassung 1808* (Innsbruck: Universitätsverlag Wagner, 1985), p. 268.

142 See Speck, Dieter, *Kleine Geschichte Vorderösterreichs* (Karlsruhe: Der Kleine Buch Verlag, 2016), p. 102.

143 Schnitzer, Casimir, *Die Kirche des heiligen Vigilius und ihre Hirten; Kurze Geschichte des Bisthums und der Bischöfe von Trient* (Bozen/Bolzano: Joseph Eberle, 1825), Band 1, p. 272.

144 "Het herzog Sigmund mit den Sungowern und Brisgowern furtruckt, als her Friedrich Gappler begert, so was Venedig gewunnen, wan sie hant sich in der stat Venedig in die Flucht bereit." Quoted from Vulpinus, Theodor, *Ritter Friedrich Kappler, Ein Elsässischer Feldhauptmann aus dem 15. Jahrhundert* (Strassburg: Heitz, 1896), p. 68.

The Tirolean Army's march home.
Illustration: Sascha Lunyakov

Roberto da Sanseverino

The aristocratic Sanseverino family belonged to the so-called "Seven Great Houses of the Kingdom of Naples", along with the Acquaviva, Celano, Evoli, Marzano, Molise und Ruffo. They were considered the leading families among the just mentioned lineages and traced their ancestry to a Norman nobleman name Turgisio. The Sanseverinos had a semi-sovereign status in the Kingdom of Naples that was repeatedly confirmed by the kings. Residing primarily in southern Italy, the widely dispersed family held 40 counties, nine margraveships, twelve duchies and ten principalities.

Roberto, da Sanseverino, Count of Caiazzo, was born in 1418. He was the son of Leonetto Sanseverino and Elisa Sforza, the sister of Francesco Sforza, the Duke of Milano. He received the honorary name "d'Aragona" from the King of Naples. Roberto, da Sanseverino fought as a condottiere in the service of the Milanese dukes in the 1440s and 1430s. In 1458 he departed on a pilgrimage to the Holy Land. After his return, he went into the King of Naples' service during the first "barons' conspiracy" (*congiura dei baroni*) from 1459 to 1462. Then he fought for Florence against Venice, after that again in Milan's service. After the murder of Galeazzo Maria Sforza, he returned to Milan. He became the bitter enemy of Milan's chancellor, Cicco Simonetta, and was forced into exile (just like Ludovico Sforza). He was sentenced in absentia to death, and his lands were confiscated and turned over to Ercole d'Este. Afterwards, Sanseverino became the Captain General of Genoa and fought against Milan in 1478. In 1479 he was allowed to return there. He also received back his properties. In 1482 he entered Venice's service and fought in the Ferrara War. In 1484 Sanseverino was named the General Captain of the Italian League for a period of nine years, which came with an annual salary of 120,000 ducats. In 1485 he received authorization to fight in the Pope's service against the Neapolitans. The campaign did not develop as hoped, and Sanseverino was dismissed by the Pope. With his first wife, Giovanna da Correggio, he had four sons who all became condottieri, and a daughter. With his second wife, Elisabetta da Montefeltro, he had another eight children, of whom his son Frederico later became a Cardinal.

According to Spreti, Vittorio, *Enciclopedia storico–nobiliare italiana: famiglie nobili e titolate viventi riconosciute dal R. Governo d'Italia, compresi: città, comunità, mense vescovili, abazie, parrocchie ed enti nobili e titolati riconosciuti* (Rome: Spreti, 1928–1936).

THE AFTERMATH

The "Council of Ten" in Venice sentenced Mattea Collalto to lifelong banishment to Crete in 1489.[145]

The Tirolean nobility were fed up with the degree of mismanagement. The Archduke had to grant the Landtag (in November 1487 in Meran) new "Court and Land Laws" ("*Hof- und Landesordnung*").

Whoever had thought that the old counselors would admit their defeat and accept their dismissal was disappointed. They knew their unstable Archduke so exactly and hoped to be restored to their old positions. They developed an active game of intrigue and turned to all the possible influential personalities. This process was not completely hopeless: Oswald von Thierstein had already been dismissed from his post as the Steward in the Alsace in the winter of 1486-87 and replaced by Wilhelm von Rappoltstein. But Archduke Sigismund had him reinstated after a few months.

Then Kaiser Fredrick III intervened, adeptly blaming Sigismund's advisors and officials, the "bad counselors" ("*bösen Räte*"),[146] for the Archduke's last escapades. At the last part of the Middle Ages, it was a common theme that the sovereign was always benevolent, wise and just. Poor decisions were often traced to bad advice from counselors. Then Kaiser Frederick III exploited this and disempowered the old court chamber once and for all and did so with the complete concurrence of the Tirolean estates. In Innsbruck on 8 January 1488, Kaiser Frederick imposed an imperial ban on various persons within Sigismund's circle of advisors.[147] Namely it included: Count Jörg von Werdenberg-Sargans; Steward *(Vogt)* Gaudenz von Matsch, Count of Kirchberg; Count Oswald von Thier-

---

145 See Shaw, Christine, *The politics of exile in Renaissance Italy* (Cambridge: Cambridge University Press, 2004), p. 100.

146 Then one cannot think of the term "*Rat*" (counsel or council) in the sense of members of the ducal council or cabinet. Court officials were called "*Räte*." Not all of them had a lot of influence in the function of their office. It was much more their position in the favor of the very gullible Archduke that gave them influence. Some advisors survived the fall of the "bad councilors" (*"bösen Räte)* and even the change of the regime. Court Marshal Paul von Liechtenstein occupied that position also under Maximilian; Georg Gossembrot climbed to be one of Maximilian's most important advisors.

147 See Messner, Florian; Ollesch, Detlef; Seehase, Hagen and Vaucher, Thomas, *Der Engadiner Krieg, Eine Reise in die Renaissance* (Eltville: RWM-Kompendium, 2016), pp. 58–59.

stein; Count Heinrich the Younger von Fürstenberg; Freiherr Hans Werner von Zimmern; Hans von Wehingen [148]; Gotthard Hartlieb; Christian Winkler; Jakob Streyt; Paul Marquart; Thomas Pipperle and Anna Spiess and their followers and accomplices for insulting His Imperial Majesty. They had committed this *"crimen leasae maiestati"* [149] in that they had convinced Archduke Sigismund that he, the Kaiser, wanted to depose Archduke Sigismund, even more, to poison him. Some of those who had fallen under the imperial ban went to Bavaria for safety, others went to Switzerland. [150] The head of the Empire's actions were actually also aimed at his Tirolean relative Sigismund. In a letter written the summer of 1487, the Kaiser had already threatened Sigismund with serious consequences if he should sell or lease Tirol to the Bavarian Duke. The Tyrolian estates, who previously were completely keen on Tirol's independence, and in no way ill-disposed toward Sigismund, were now open to new arrangements due to the mismanagement and the counselors' conduct.

The Kaiser made an agreement with the Tirolean estates that upon Archduke Sigismund's death, his son King Maximilian [151] should become the new sovereign. The nobles rejected his rule (he was opposed to their lifelong right to live in their castles and to fish and hunt anywhere in Tirol). And there was an appropriate appanage for good measure. [152]

In the abdication letter of 1490, it stated that Sigismund resigned based on his "age and dim-wittedness", which gives a true picture of the ruler's mental condition. Sigismund's final wish before he died was to again dip his hands into silver coins. Three bowls filled with coins were brought to his bedside. But the 400 guilders had to be borrowed - that was how impoverished Sigismund the Rich-in-Coin was at the end of his life. That is how he died in Innsbruck on 4 March 1496. Archduke Sigismund was buried next to his first wife in the family crypt in Stams in an ostentatious ceremony. His widow, the just-turned-28-years-old Katharina, wed Maximilian's comrade-in-arms and confidant, Duke Erich of Brunswick, in a second marriage.

Sigismund's former advisor Oswald von Thierstein had already died in 1488. His brother Wilhelm became his heir.

Nikolaus von Firmian became Tirol's new Captain of the Land (*Landeshauptmann*) in 1488, and in 1495, Maximilian appointed him to be the head of the court (*Hofmeister*) for his wife Bianca Maria Sforza.

Gaudenz von Matsch obtained citizenship in Lucerne and tried to escape from the imperial ban. He did succeed, in that finally in December 1496, he sold some properties (Castels and Schiers) in the Prättigau region to King Maximilian, [153] but he forfeited any political influence in Tirol. He died on 24 April 1504 at the Churburg Castle. [154] After the imposition of the imperial ban, Count Jörg von Werdenberg-Sargans trend to establish an alliance against the Habsburgs between the Swiss and Bavaria and another between the Swiss and Venice. He died in 1504, ruined politically and financially, as the last representative of his house. He left behind six illegitimate children.

Friedrich Kappler had an impressive military career. He received honors and financial awards. On 27 December 1487 he was again in Tirol, based on the Innsbruck "*Raitbuch*" (ledger) of 1487, where it reads:

"To Friedrich K., knights and men, who were under him in the field 27 Dec. 1,500 guilders and Friedrich. K. of late on 24 Dec. 100, on 27 Dec. 21 guilders 4 pfennigs B. and on 24 Dec. to his scribe 12 guilders."

Additionally, he received a payment of grace ("*Gnadengeld*") of 1,500 guilders, and after his return to his homeland of Alsace, the Stewardship of Maasmünster (Masevaux, FR) and the village of Gildweiler (Gildwiller, FR).

On 14 January 1493, as the commander of Habsburg forces, he defeated a French expeditionary corps at Dournon. In 1495, he commanded, jointly with Georg von Ebenstein, a contingent of Austrian mercenaries in the service of Milanese Duke Ludovico Sforza against the French. [155] In the 1499 Swiss War, he was one of the few commanders on the Austrian side whose reputations was not damaged. On 1 June 1499, Kappler led his forces to victory over the Swiss in an action at Altkirch.

Then on 22 July 1499, came the Habsburgs' disastrous defeat by the Swiss at Dornach an der Birs, in which Kappler commanded the forces from the Sundgau and barely escaped with his life. In 1500, he was the Württemberg steward (*Landvogt*) in Mömpelgart (Montbeliard, FR). In 1504 and 1505 he commanded the Württemberg cavalry in the Landshut War of Succession. Friedrich Kappler died

---

148 He had been the senior Marshal and had had a significant part in the decision to go to war against Venice.

149 The crime of injured sovereignty or "High treason against a sovereign" or "*lèse-majesté* crime". A *crimen laesae maiestatis* could include such acts as espionage.

150 It appears there was some upset among the Alsatian knights over Thierstein's dismissal. In 1488, Archduke Sigismund wrote to Friedrich Kappler, Wilhelm Kappler, Martin Stör and other Alsatian notables that should not let Thierstein instigate against him (Sigismund) and they should continue to faithfully fulfill their duties as vassals.

151 He had been the Roman King since 1486.

152 Nevertheless, he died almost pennyless.

153 His daughter Catharina married Maximilian's chamberlain, Erhard von Polheim. Catharina was designated as his primary heir. After her death in 1514, there was a decades-long legal battle about the inheritance between Polheim and the Count von Trapp, the nephew of Gaudenz von Matsch, which the latter won in the end. See Messner; Ollesch; Seehase and Vaucher, *Der Engadiner Krieg*, p. 71.

154 See Ladurner, *Die Vögte von Matsch*, p. 154.

155 See Messner, Florian and Seehase, Hagen, *Die Enntbirgischen Feldzüge* (Berlin: Zeughaus, 2018), p. 61.

in the Alsatian Maasmünster in January 1506. Kappler was married twice and had two daughters, Magdalena and Clarelse.

Antonio Maria da Sanseverino recovered from his wounds, was captured by the Tiroleans, and got free again in September 1487. He died in Milan in 1509, as a veteran of many campaigns. Johann von Waldburg-Sonnenberg later became the Steward (*Truchsess*) of Waldburg and died in Wolfegg on 24 June 1510.

The church in the Kauner Valley (*Kaunertal*), a side valley of the Upper Inn Valley (*Oberinntal*) gained great importance for the Landsknechts. According to passed down history, the first small chapel was built in the 13th century by the knight Erbo Schenkenberg as penitence for a murder. In 1483, Archduke Sigismund endowed a chaplain. A religious picture from the 14th century made the church into a place of pilgrimage for the Landsknechts.

In memory of the Tirolean (noble) participants in the battle, the "Calliano Victory Plaques" ("*Callianer Siegestafeln*") were hung in Trento.[156] The participants in the 1487 campaign mentioned, were named as follows:[157]

Friedrich Kappler
Christoph von Hattstatt
Hans Kaspar von Laubenberg
Ludwig von Rechberg
Ludwig von Reinach
Hans Schinhais
Martin Stör
Pangraz Han von Hanberg
Georg Kreuzer von Werdenberg
Thomas von Freundsberg
Wilhelm Kappler (a brother of Friedrich Kappler)
Heinrich von Hattstatt
Philipp von Lichtenstein
Simon Pfirt
Hans von Freiberg
Hans von Hirschberg
Hans von Neuburg
Hermann Waldner
Hans von Rinn
Hans von Weinegg
Georg von Welsberg
Michael von Hecken
Ludwig von Blumau
Karins von Neufels
Georg von Riedberg
Georg von Ebenstain
Georg von Zwingenstein
Caspar Pöcklin
Hans First

Friedrich von Knöringen
Werner Giel von Gielsberg
Melchior Brandeck
Hans von Hohenfirst
Fritz von Winkenthal
Hans Anich
Michael Anich
Veit Anich
Claus Murer
Ludwig Müller[158]

Today the Calliano Victory Plaques have unfortunately disappeared. However, Roberto da Sanseverino d´Aragona's armor is still on hand: It is kept in the Viennese Armor Chamber (*Wiener Rüstkammer*). The armor that belonged to his son, Antonio Maria, was brought by Johann von Waldburg-Sonnenberg, the duel's victor, to Swabia (where he also founded a chapel). In the Trento Cathedral, one can still view Sanseverino's (senior's) tomb slab: It shows the commander in the prime of his life. In his right hand he holds Venice's banner, but with the shaft broken, the Lion of St. Mark lies at his feet.

In St. Katherine's Church (*St. Katharinenkirche*) in Wolfegg, one can see the memorial fresco begun in 1735 by Franz Joseph Spiegler, which shows a phase of the duel. In the Waldburg Castle, there is a baroque painting also depicting the duel.

The Innsbruck Court Church (*Innsbrucker Hofkirche*) contains Kaiser Maximilian I's monumental tomb. An inscription refers to the Tiroleans' victory at Calliano. The Imperial Secretary Georg Boczkay, who proposed the inscription for Maximilian's cenotaph, described the historical issue thusly: *"IVNCTIS CVM PATRVELE SIGISMVNDO ARMIS, ROVERETVM OPPIDVM EXPVGNATVM, AC VENETORVM COPIAE VNACVM DVCE ROBERTO SANSEVERINO, AD VICVM CALLIANVM DELETAE."* In English it means "After the forces[159] had joined with Uncle Sigismund, the town of Rovereto was captured, and the Venetians' army with its leader Roberto da Sanseverino was crushed at the village of Calliano." Undoubtably the writer of these lines intended to tell of Kaiser Maximilian's fame and achievements at the Battle of Calliano in a positive light for posterity, since this does not correspond to evident historic facts. Maximilian was not at all involved in this conflict, the entire undertaking completely contradicted the intentions and policies of the Imperial House of Habsburg.

---

156 It also could have been a victory plaque that later broke into two pieces. The plaques were still there and the names readable in the 19th century.

157 As shown by Hormayr, *Taschenbuch für vaterländische Geschichte*, p. 352.

158 Most of those specifically named came from the Upper Alsace (*Oberelsass*) or from Tirol.

159 This is meant as King Maximilian's forces.

Waldburg Castle, Photo: Henrik Seehase

Venetian footsoldiers in armor
The quality of the weaponry and the armor reflects Venice's wealth.
Photo: Città del Grifo

WARFARE AT THE TIME OF THE ROVERETO WAR

The Tirolean Forces

In his rhymed chronicle, Michel Beheim describes an event that occurred on 4 August 1471. A military force from the Kurpfalz (Palatine Electorate) succeeded in capturing the town of Lambsheim in the Frankenthal (valley); in the 1,389th verse of Beheim's chronicle it says that among Lambsheim's defenders were 20 "foot soldiers from the same land". Either this refers to the same regional origin of these foot soldiers and the men-at-arms (*Reisiger*) or it is actually the first mention of the term "*Landsknechte*".[160]

However, they were not the Landsknechts in the sense of type of soldiers associated with Kaiser/King Maximilian or Georg von Frundsberg. The year 1487, with two militarily historic battles, specifically showed the genesis of this new kind of war fighter. Along with the Battle of Calliano, this was the Battle of Stoke in England on 13 June 1487. Besides rebellious English nobles with their followers and several thousand lightly armed Irish, there were 2,000 Swiss and German mercenaries under Captain Martin Schwarz, who formed an army that wanted to depose the new English king, Henry VII, from the House of Tudor, in the name of a pretender to the throne from the rival House of York. Despite their bravery and despite the new (to England) method of fighting, the mercenary unit was destroyed along with its captain Schwarz[161] and his deputy and standard-bearer ("*Venner*"), Hans Kuttler from Bern.[162] They had been recruited in Mecheln, the property of Margareta of York, the widow of Charles the Bold. She was from the House of York and her court was the meeting place for many supporters of that family. Along with the political, the military aspect was important.

The Swiss had been considered Europe's best infantry even before the Burgundian Wars. One must distinguish between the regular units of the Swiss "*Orte*" (cantons or "*lieues*") and the bands of volunteers who often, without approval (or even against expressed orders), went into the service of those who could pay large wages. Starting in the mid-15th century, Swiss mercenaries seem to have been ubiquitous in the surrounding countries. For example, Swiss foot soldiers under the command of the later mayor of Zurich, Hans Waldmann, demonstrated their fighting worth in the service of Elector Friedrich of the Pfalz in the Battle of Seckenheim on 30 June 1462. However, that was with the concurrence of the Swiss Confederation, being recruited by the Elector of the Pfalz, who had developed good relations with them. Not a lot is known about the 200 Swiss fighters who were recruited during the Second Margraves' War[163] by the city of Augsburg to fight on the side of Margrave Albrecht III Achilles of Brandenburg-Ansbach.[164] He had once had bad experiences with the Swiss. In the First Margraves' War, his forces had suffered a defeat at Pillenreuther Weihern on 11 March 1450 against the city levy of Nuremberg that consisted of horsemen and 4,000 foot soldiers, among whom were 800 to 1,000 Swiss with long pikes. Their captain, Erich Malters, was named the commander of all Nuremberg's foot soldiers. He wanted to arm the Nurembergers similarly to the Swiss fashion, not with short pikes, but with halberds, hand cannons (culverins) and crossbows. Together with the Swiss with their long pikes, he could form a solid, square infantry formation ("*Gevierthaufen*"). But Malters did not dismiss using a wagon fort (*Wagenburg* or laager).[165] The Swiss were even represented in the Burgundian Army. In the contingent that was commanded by the Steward of the Leased Lands (*Vogt der Pfandländer*), Peter of Hagenbach, in the 1472 campaign against France, there were along with a relatively unclear number of horsemen, 275 foot soldiers with long range weapons, 67 with halberds, plus 322 with long pikes. In addition to the French region of Auxois[166] and Montagne-Noire cited as their regions of origin, were the County of Pfirt (Ferrette) and Switzerland.

---

160 Twenty "*Fußknecht derselben Land*". The term "Landsknecht" ("*Landsknechte*") first shows up in writing in the Prussian chronicle written by Johann von Posilge at the beginning of the 15th century.

161 Schwarz was a veteran of the Burgundian War, was supposedly knighted by the Kaiser for his actions at the siege of Neuss. He had not - as claimed many times – fought in the Duke of Burgundy's army, but in the Imperial Army. Later he belonged to the army of 6,000 men "from upper German lands, from Swabia and from Swiss parts" ("*uß oberdütschen Landen, von Schwaben und Schwyzeren glych Theil*") that moved to Flanders . In 1485, he commanded a unit of 200 Swiss soldiers in the service of Count Engelbert of Nassau. See Anshelm, Valerius, *Berner Chronik*, Erster Band (1st Vol.) (Bern: L.A. Haller, 1825, p. 390.

162 He was banished from his homeland – supposedly because of unauthorized participation in a campaign that was not officially approved.

163 This was the drawn-out conflict from 1460 to 1463 between Margrave Albrecht III Achilles of Brandenburg-Ansbach and Duke Ludwig IX of Bayern-Landshut and their respective allies.

164 See Weissinger, Rolf, *Die Schlacht bei Giengen, 19. Juli 1462, Die Geschichte eines vergessenen Krieges* (Stuttgart: KLIO Baden-Württemberg, 1998), p. 18.

165 See Nell, *Die Landsknechte*, p. 15. Long pikes are not the subject in this context. Obviously one could not train men properly in their use in a short period.

166 This region belonged to the Burgundian core lands at that time.

In case of war, the cantons' levies[167] could be accompanied by bands of volunteers, under their own captains, that had to provision themselves but exploited the opportunity to take booty.[168]

The Swiss, that is to say those from the Confederation as well as residents from the associated *Orte*, left the limits of their homelands to go to war and did so also when there was no obligation to the alliance. Actually, they were always ready to go to war. Each of them practiced handling weapons starting in his youth, but there was hardly any organized military training.[169] In the Swiss Confederation's youth associations, handling weapons was a top-level sport.[170] The principle of universal military duty applied from the age of 14 (later 16) years to 60 years. The *Tagsatzung*, a kind of Parliament, with delegates from the individual Swiss *Orte* (cantons) determined the number of armed men and the cantonal leadership organized the mobilization. That is how the numerical superiority of the Swiss armies at that time can be explained. But often the Swiss attacked when they were numerically smaller, even when the numeric ratios were decidedly to their disadvantage (for example in 1444 against the Armagnacs).[171] Their complete military readiness, great bravery and warlike attitude were hallmarks of the Swiss.[172] So the simple Swiss soldier went into battle with his weapons, with the intent of having ruthless offensive effect. The weapons were the halberd, which had to be swing with two hands, a sword, dagger and axe. Long-range weapons were not widely used, but still played a certain role. Not much store was put in armor, at least initially. Logically for the pikemen, who were employed in larger numbers, protective armor was needed. The principle was that each Swiss fighting man was responsible for providing his own equipment, but the extent depended on his finances. Poor men received what they needed for war from the arsenal. If a man had debts, his creditor could not take away his weapons. If someone wanted to gain citizenship in one of the Confederation's cities, he had to definitely prove that he owned appropriate military equipment. The cantons' levies were divided into the "*Auszug*" ("move-out" - as a rule, it included mostly unmarried men 16 to 30 years old), the *Landwehr* (those who were a little older), and in the direst emergencies, the *Landsturm*. The cantons with a large urban population (like Zurich) organized their city dwellers according to guilds.

In the Burgundian Wars, the Swiss infantry showed its tremendous impact. The tactical formation was the 30 to 50-man wide and similarly deep phalanx ("*Gewalthaufen*"). The exterior ranks were made up of experienced men with 5.5 to 6-meter long pikes. The Swiss held their long pike (whose shaft was slightly conical) at the balance point, i.e., about a third of the way from the bottom. W\with leveled pikes, the points of those in the fourth rank protruded a half meter beyond the foremost rank.[173] The Swiss had painfully experienced the effect of the long pike at their defeat by the Milanese at the 1422 Battle of Arbedo and promptly adopted it into their own arsenal, where it gradually supplemented and replaced the halberd. A sculpture from 1370 from Basel (which did not yet belong to the Confederation) shows a soldier with such a long pike.[174] Not many kinds of wood were suitable for producing the shafts for the long pikes, so it was the wood from the cornel cherry tree, and later the vertically strong ash, which was used frequently.[175]

The pikemen were equipped with half armor. In the middle of the formation stood men with halberds, other pole arms like bills ("*Roßschindern*" -"horse flayers"), glaives, voulges, guisarmes, Lucerne hammers and so forth. Those wielding the long pikes stopped enemy cavalry and drove back enemy infantry, then those with halberds broke out of the center of the formation and engaged in the hand-to-hand combat. Around 1400, 80 percent of the Swiss infantry was armed with halberds, and at Murten in 1476 it was still about 40 percent. A strong thrust with this weapon could even penetrate plate armor.[176] Equally feared were the fighters with the two-hander sword. They were most often select men who had to demonstrate their ability with the weapon to a fencing instructor. They received double pay and were frequently the bodyguard for the commander or guarded the flag. Along with that, the Swiss sword (*Schweizerschwert*) and Swiss rapier (*Schweizerdegen*) were in use, which differed in the length and width of their blades. Fencing schools, after the German model, became popular in the Swiss Confederation. For example, in 1454, the renowned fencing instructor Hans Talhoffer stayed in Zurich and gave fencing lessons in the town hall square (*Rathausplatz*).

Cavalry did not play an important role with the Swiss - only Bern had a "horse banner" ("*Rossbanner*") with 100 armored horsemen with lances and 200 lightly armed, mounted men.

---

167 These were divided into the "*Auszug*" ("move-out" - as a rule, it included mostly unmarried men 16 to 30 years old), the *Landwehr* (those who were a little older), and in the direst emergencies, the *Landsturm*. See Miller, Douglas and Embleton, Gerry, *The Swiss at War, 1300–1500* (London: Osprey, 1979), p. 4.

168 See Fiedler, Siegfried, *Taktik und Strategie der Landsknechte, 1500–1650* (Augsburg: Bechtermünz, 2002), pp. 30–31. These bands of volunteer had not taken oaths and did not receive regular pay.

169 See Schaufelberger, Walter, *Der alte Schweizer und sein Krieg* (Zurich: Europa Verlag,1966), p. 43.

170 See Fiedler, *Taktik und Strategie der Landsknechte*, p. 40.

171 See Keegan, John, *Die Kultur des Krieges* (Berlin: Rowohl, 1965), p. 467.

172 See Fiedler, *Taktik und Strategie der Landsknechte*, p. 30.

173 See Ortenburg, Georg, *Waffen der Landsknechte, 1500–1650* (Augsburg: Bechtermünz / Verlagsgruppe Weltbild , 2002), p. 45.

174 See Heath, *Armies of the Middle Ages*, p. 136.

175 This occurred very frequently in northern Italy.

176 See Ortenburg, *Waffen der Landsknechte*, p. 45.

The Thurgau, southern Swabian and Bavarian soldiers' appearance was still largely influenced by the Swiss examples.
Photo: Fred Wutz

The long-range weapons used by the Swiss were the crossbow and the handheld firearm; the longbow played only a marginal role. Around the middle of the 15th century, the ratio of crossbowmen to hand-gunners was 8:1; at the time of the Burgundian Wars, it was still only 1:1. It is certain that 800 Swiss hand-gunners were present at the Battle of Nancy in 1477.

The participation of Swiss mercenaries also had an impact in the military conflicts in the southern German area, for example, at the 1462 Battle of Seckenheim.

The Habsburgs and others had to very painfully experience the Swiss' military way of war. The Habsburgs were not always standing on the opposing side. It must be noted that during the Burgundian Wars, within the large Swiss armies, there were also contingents from allied and confederated districts ("*zugewandte Orte*") and the "Common Domains" ("*gemeine Herrschaften*") that fought alongside. About 30 percent of the Swiss and allied armies at the Battle of Grandson consisted of fighters from the mentioned territories, which provided the majority of the cavalry, but also part of the infantry[177]. There were also 60 foot soldiers from Nördlingen (under Captain Gabriel Ehringer) in the Allies' ranks.[178]

During the Burgundian Wars in the Basel contingent there were many Swiss mercenaries; the Basel men (in contrast to many Alsatian troops and other units) enjoyed the respect of the Swiss ("but the city of Basel has good men" - "*aber die statt Basel haby guot lüt*").

Many protagonists in the Rovereto War and its lead-up in Tirol were veterans of the Burgundian Wars: Friedrich Kappler, Bernhard Gradner, Oswald von Thierstein, Conrad Gächuff and others.

The unreconcilable antagonism that the Swiss "*Reisläufer*" (hired infantrymen) and Landsknechts had against one another was a phenomenon of later days. In 1487, many Swiss mercenaries fought in the ranks of the Tirolean army: the mercenaries of Ulrich VII of Hohensax, like the men whom Conrad Gächuff had recruited in the Thurgau and in the old Confederation. People from Basel were represented in the army, likewise fighters from Graubünden's regions that provided levies to Gaudenz von Matsch's units. However, the latter, along with their leader, turned their backs on the campaign before the decisive battle of Calliano.

The influences of the Swiss military system on the surrounding territories, especially on the Habsburg lands, had already begun before the Burgundian Wars. And it was not the Swiss who were the first instructors within Maximilian's forces in Flanders who took care of having the non-Swiss adopt the Swiss model.

It seems tragic that of all things the later King and Kaiser Maximilian, who not only highly valued the Swiss activities in his army, but also who had the greatest respect for the warlike qualities of the Swiss, had little love for the cantonal leadership.[179] In March 1488, Kaiser Frederick III[180] demanded forces from the Abbott[181] of the St. Gallen Monastery for a campaign to Flanders (from February to May 1488, Maximilian was held prisoner by Flemish rebels in Bruges). In reaction, the Abbott turned to the allied Confederation for advice. The Swiss advised the Abbott that he should only send the absolute minimum that was his duty as an imperial prince. Even more than the Swiss tendencies against the head of the empire, it was actually the payments by foreign powers to the Swiss "pension lords" ("*Pensionsherren*") that caused the attitude. High-ranking personalities of the individual Swiss *Orte* received bribes ("*Zuwendungen*") that were intended to ensure a particular political direction. In this, the Milanese dukes were more adept than the Habsburgs, and the French Crown's actions were especially successful. Then one or another of the Confederation *Orte* or the *Tagsatzung* (assembly) as a whole issued a prohibition against being hired by a particular party to a conflict. After a temporary high, recruitment in Switzerland by the Habsburgs became more difficult shortly after the Burgundian Wars.[182] Nevertheless, Swiss *Reisläufer* and Landsknechts fought side-by-side with the Habsburgs during the 1490 Hungarian campaign. A somewhat later chronicler from St. Gallen,

---

177 The allied and dependent territories stood up the following contingents:
 Fribourg: 828 men,
 Biel: 213 men,
 Solothurn: 928 men,
 St.Gallen (city): 131 men,
 St.Gallen (Abbey): 151 men,
 Baden: 286 men,
 Schaffhausen: 106 men,
 Appenzell: 200 men.
 The units from the Lower Union (Niedere Vereinigung) were organized as follows:
 Basel: 1,200 men,
 Strasbourg: 259 men,
 Colmar: 35 men,
 Schlettstadt (Sélestat): 26 men,
 Rottweil: 100 men,
 The *Waldstädte*, the Sundgau and the Black Forest (Schwarzwald) districts: 1,500 men.

178 See Würdinger, Joseph, *Kriegsgeschichte von Bayern, Franken, Pfalz und Schwaben*, Erster Band, (Munich: Cotta'sche Buchhandlung, 1868), p. 130.

179 On 14 September 1487, King Maximilian was still able to renew the alliance with Zurich, Bern, Uri, Unterwalden (Obwalden and Nidwalden, the core lands), Zug with the external office, Freiburg im Uechtland (Fribourg) and Solothurn.

180 He remained an lifelong opponent of the Swiss, he had not recognized the "Perpetual Accord" ("*Ewige Richtung*").

181 Abbot Ulrich Rösch.

182 Still in 1498 Hans Conrad von Rümlang recruited Swiss mercenaries for a planned campaign by King Maximilian's planned campaign in Burgundy against France. Rümlang was the lord of Alt-Wülflingen, a citizen of Winterthur and married to an illegitimate daughter of Archduke Sigismund. He supposedly took part in the first Hegau action in the 1499 Swabian War. In 1529 he was executed in Zurich for forging documents. See Messner; Ollesch; Seehase and Vaucher: *Der Engadiner Krieg*, p. 66.

Watt, reported "in this campaign, there were many *Eidgenossen* [Confederates] and also some from our town of St. Gallen with the Landsknechts." [183]

Naturally the Swiss were offended when their martial pride was challenged. Conrad Gächuff's loudmouthed announcement that he could train a Swabian so well in the use of the pike that the fighter he taught would later be worth two Swiss, was more an indicator of his own capabilities as a military organizer. In 1486, the Confederation's *Tagsatzung* took up the matter of this speech, [184] which it took as defaming the Swiss warrior's ethos. Despite this, he was able to recruit troops within the Confederation and particularly within the "Common Domain" ("*gemeine Herrschaft*") of Thurgau for the campaign against Venice. At the assembly in Constance, the Swiss complained about the foreign (southern German) fighters who were claiming to be Swiss, which damaged the real Swiss reputation. [185]

It is hardly surprising that there were attempts in southern Germany to create infantry of equal value to that of the Swiss. However, it remained just an attempt until the German Landsknechts appeared under King (and later Kaiser) Maximilian). [186]

In the mid-15th century north of the upper Rhine and Lake Constance, there were small unions of foot soldiers who would happily hire themselves out to predatory nobles. [187] They were not militarily significant, but they demonstrated organizational forms and structures that one observed later with the Landsknechts. A group of Swiss renegades left the impression, more as a legend than a reality, that they had nested themselves in the Hohenkrähen Castle in Hegau after the "Old Zurich War" ("*Alter Zürichkrieg*") of 1440-1446. But that band was unjustifiably identified with a Zurich noble family that had played a leading political role during the "Old Zurich War".

In 1476, during the campaign against Durk Charles the Bold to retake Lorraine, a 400-man strong unit of Alsatian infantry ran directly into a Burgundian attack and was scattered without effort. The Flemish pikemen, who had been a standard part of the Burgundian army and then went to war against France on the side of Prince Maximilian (the new husband of Maria of Burgundy [188]), were of a different caliber. Maximilian could rely on the expertise of two renown commanders. [189] Jacques de Romont, Count of Savoy and Count Engelbert of Nassau, who was just ransomed free for 50,000 guilders from being the city of Strasbourg's prisoner of war, took over command of two lance wielding infantry units, that flanked by cavalry squadrons, went up against the French at the Battle of Guinegate (on 7 August 1479). While France's mounted ordinance companies drove their enemies to flee, Maximilian's infantry, the so-called "*Gewalthaufen*" (phalanxes), advanced and claimed the battlefield. However, afterward, the army fell apart. Maximilian, who had fought (on foot!) as a pikeman at the Battle of Guinegate [190] (7 August 1479), liked the idea of infantry who were nationally homogenous, motivated by high ideals, and who fought by the Swiss model. But this still had to be created. In 1486, the year Maximilian was elected the Roman King, he had assembled two such units. Each with 3,000 to 4,000 men armed with long pikes, were made ready for combat by their Swiss instructors. Like some of the units raised later, their members came from Swabia, the Alsace, and the Rhineland as well as Tirol. Contingents from these regions had already fought alongside the Swiss during the Burgundian Wars. For example, in early 1476, the town of Rottweil had sent several dozen hand-gunners to aid Basel; at the Battle of Murten there were still 50 men from Rottweil.

The German Landsknechts and the Swiss *Reisläufers'* distinctive identifying features served as signs differentiating them. This difference between the two groups, which was occasionally deadly, did not exist yet – at least not to the extent it did in later decades. Some of these characteristics were already very pronounced on the Swiss side. For example, the cross slashed into the gambeson, carrying the Swiss dagger, and use of a hand-and-a-half sword with a narrow blade [191] had long been signs of the Swiss. The identifying features clearly associated with the Landsknechts could have been inspired in the early phase by the Swiss, before they were modified later as differentiating characteristics. [192]

Landsknechts were already represented at the Battles of Calliano and Stoke, and their numbers would grow rapidly within the next years. Within the scope of the Venetian War as a whole, the feudal levy and the town or city

---

183 Quote as "*in disem zug sind bey den lanzknechten vil Eidgenossen und auch ettlich uss unser Stat S. Gallen gsin*" in Delbrück, Hans, *Geschichte der Kriegskunst im Rahmen der politischen Geschichte*, Band 4(Berlin: George Stilke & Walter de Gruyter, 1920), p. 12.

184 Something like this could quickly lead one to the gallows.

185 See Nell, *Die Landsknechte*, p. 169.

186 See Kramer, Daniel Robert, *Das Söldnerwesen, Militärisches Unternehmertum in der Genese des internationalen Systems* (Wiesbaden: Springer Vorschau, 2010), p. 45.

187 In 1388 in Swabia there were some bands of independent foot soldiers who hired themselves out to towns as mercenaries, and one such band called itself the "*Freiharst*".

188 She was the daughter and heir of Burgundian Duke Charles the Bold who died at the Battle of Nancy at the beginning of 1477.

189 Both had shortly before been in the service of Duke Charles the Bold.

190 Today called Enguinegatte.

191 The typical Landsknecht's sword, the so-called „Katzbalger" ("cat tussler") showed up soon. It was however, also gladly used by the Swiss *Reisläufers* (as booty?). See Bächtiger, Franz, up you "Bemerkungen zum Widersacher des Eidgenossen von 1529" in *Zeitschrift für schweizerische Archäologie und Kunstgeschichte*, Band 37, (Bern, 1980), pp. 252–259, here: p. 253.

192 But that is speculative. Landsknechts later wore berets with feathers pointing toward the front, while the Swiss *Reisläufer*'s berets' feathers pointed to the rear.. A typical Landsknecht pose was bracing the right hand on his back, while the *Reisläufer* supported his hand on his right hip. See ibid. p. 253.

For soldiers using long pikes, maintaining the formation required a lot of practice.
Photo: Arma Georgii/Fred Wutz

militias, like that of Trento, played a minor yet important role.[193] The town and city infantry was organized based on guilds. The urban militias were organized by quarters, around sections of the town/city walls and towers that they could effectively defend. Each quarter was overseen by a "*Viertelmeister*" ("quarter master") named by the town/city council. This "quarter master" sometimes also had civil duties like firefighting and oversight of the market. Frequently the "quarter master" was also the bearer of the banner (in the sense of a "*Bannerherr*" or captain). Then in the southwest he was called the "*Venner*" (like the Swiss way[194]). He was assisted by other officers, semiprofessional gatekeepers, trumpeters and (starting at the end of the 14th century) by a master gunsmith ("*Büchsenmeister*). Rarely were all of a city's able-bodied men called up; that actually occurred in case of a direct attack on the town/city walls. The choice of men to be provided was up to the towns themselves, in rural villages it was up to the "*Pfleger*" (or often the judge), in a manor it was up to the lord of the manor who was often represented by one of his officials. In the southern German region there was no established system for military service[195] for free peasants, with the minor exception of the "*Hauensteiner Landfahnen*" ("Hauenstein Country Flags") in the Black Forest. However, this *Hauensteiners* were said to be relatively poorly armed (just with halberds) and equipped. During the time of the Burgundian Wars, the *Landfahnen* are reported to have had 1,000 men. In Tirol, the land whose later riflemen were so highly respected, the military obligation of the estates was already traceable to the beginning of the 14th century.[196] A fundamental prerequisite for this was having a large number of free peasants. In any case, initially these levies of peasants were only one (and not the most important) pillar along with the armies of knights and bands of mercenaries. The "*Tiroler Landlibell*" ("Tirolean Land Libel") of 23 June 1511 first created a military structure based on peasants and burghers and was unique in the whole Empire.[197] Kaiser Maximilian, in consultation with the Tirolean estates, established that the classes had to perform wartime duty to defend the country. The *Landlibell* was part of the Tirolean constitution. All able-bodied men from the age of 18 to 60 could be called up to defend against a danger and employed within the country. Each resident was permitted to carry a weapon (the origin of the Tirolean *Schützenwesen* – Marksman System). In 1534, King Ferdinand I confirmed the peasants' right to bear arms. Peasant levies were not necessarily only armed with modified farming implements like billhooks, war scythes or war flails. However, their armament was as a rule older and/or poorer than that of the semiprofessional mercenaries.

The Tirolean "*Bergknappen*" (Mountain Youths), who showed up frequently in their own units, was a special feature. The 400 "*Knappen*" that Archduke Sigismund sent to Micheletto Segato, who fought in the Giudicarie region could have been *Reisige*[198] or actually "*Bergknappen*".

A typical weapon for the infantry was the crossbow. For the nobles, the crossbow was popular as a hunting weapon, in the towns and castles it was the weapon of choice for defending the walls. Every town and every prince wanted to get capable people to produce these weapons including the accessories.[199] In castles and the towns' defensive works, special spanning mechanisms were maintained with which it was possible to quickly span crossbows. But these mechanisms were heavy and hardly useable in mobile warfare.

At a range of 100 meters or less the effect of the crossbow was enormous, e.g., in 1488 Margrave Albrecht of Baden was shot in the neck with a crossbow bolt through his armor. Around the year 1450, the crossbow was a valued and widespread weapon. At Duke Ludwig of the Pfalz-Zweibrücken-Veldenz's mustering of a levy in 1453, only two men were armed with maces, eight with battle axes, 585 with pikes, 352 with firearms, but 1,016 with crossbows.[200] This levy was employed in an attack on the town of Mutzig in the Alsace. But the importance of the crossbow decreased in the following decades. The Frankish contingent under Margrave Albrecht Achilles of Brandenburg that participated in the Empire's 1474-75 war against Burgundy consisted of 600 horsemen and 3,000 foot soldiers. Of the latter, 40 percent had crossbows and firearms, 20 percent had pikes and 40 percent had halberds and similar weapons. In 1492, of the 1,836 of the men called up by the Governorate (*Vizdomamt*) of Straubing, 551 were hand-gunners, 950 halberdiers, 144 men with awl pikes (*Ahlspiesse*) and only 191 crossbowmen. Granted that this example was arbitrarily selected, but it does show the general development. In 1425 in Augsburg, a crossbow cost three guilder, in 1459 in Ingolstadt, 51 crossbows were bought with 115 guilders, ten cross-

---

193 Dazu konnten auch Söldner gehören, Augsburg unterhielt im Jahre 1449 1200 besoldete Trabanten mit Feuerrohren oder Armbrusten. Vgl. Würdinger: *Kriegsgeschichte von Bayern, Franken, Pfalz und Schwaben*, p. 374.

194 In Bern, for example, the bakers', smiths' tanners' and butchers' guilds provided the city's four "*Venner*".

195 In Friesland the situation was different, when one considers the Dithmarsch peasant army's victory over the Danish army of knights at Hemmingstedt in 1500.

196 See Fiedler, *Taktik und Strategie der Landsknechte*, p. 106

197 There were, however, precursor developments: The first two Tirolean defense-related laws („*Zuzugsordnungen*") were from 1478 and 1479. In Austria in the Enns and in Styria there were already similar laws since the 1430s and 1440s.

---

198 In this case, they would have belonged to the cavalry.

199 The men who produced the crossbows and those who used them were both call "*Armbruster*", the bolts were made by "*Pfeilschnitzern*" ("arrow carvers") and the quivers made from furs were made by "*Kurdaunern*".

200 See Würdinger, *Kriegsgeschichte von Bayern, Franken, Pfalz und Schwaben*, p. 77.

bow winches with 14 guilders seven *Groschen*. [201] In 1507, King Maximilian[202] issued an order for an intended campaign that no one was permitted to appear with a crossbow, but shooters were to show up with handguns.

The handheld firearms used from 1450 to 1500 can be classified as two basic types: hand cannons (*Feuerrohre*, literally "fire tubes") and matchlock muskets (*Luntenschlossmusketen*). For both types, Burgundy was the trailblazer.

The hand cannon "*Feuerrohr*",[203] represented by the famous Tannenberg gun (*Tannenbergbüchse*), essentially consisted of a smooth-bore pipe with an igniting hole at one end. It was made of iron, bronze or a copper alloy. The caliber was usually between 13 and 22 millimeters / inches (although there were also monstrous examples of up to 38mm / inches); the barrel was only a few calibers long. Often a metal bar was attached to the end that extended as a handgrip or knob; the pipe (barrel) could also be mounted on a wooden shaft (usually in the primitive shape of a round staff). Because the powder charge had to be ignited with one hand by holding a red-hot wire or a slow-burning wick to the firing hole, it left only one hand free to hold the weapon. Therefore, the weapon was usually rested on a forked support or hooked onto a parapet, and often a hook was forged onto the barrel to take up the recoil (thus the name "hook hand cannon" – "*Hakenbüchse*"). The precision of this hand cannon was not good, aiming hardly possible, and it is not possible to speak of "accuracy" in this context. To improve the employment of this weapon, often two shooters were used, one to hold the weapon, the other to ignite it. Despite the poor accuracy, hand cannons remained in use was matchlocks appeared. The matchlock was known in Italy since at least 1411. A fuse was hung on an S-shaped device ("serpentine"), that was touched into the firing pan by pressing on the other end of the serpentine. Later the serpentine was moved with a spring mechanism when a trigger was touched. This system (together with improved kinds of gunpowder that burned more uniformly) produced a more secure ignition and improved the accuracy. A rule of thumb was the weight of the powder charge should be barely half as much as the weight of the lead ball.[204]
A very fine-grained form of black powder was used, but it readily absorbed moisture. Because of the varying density of the various components, it tended to decompose in transport. Granulated powder did not have this disadvantage and it came into use with artillery pieces in this timeframe, but only began to be used for hand-fired weapons starting about 1600.[205]

Not infrequently the barrels were bundled and mounted on carts, but those were artillery weapons moved by draft horses. These so-called "organ cannons" ("Orgelgeschütze") could play a meaningful role in defending against a siege.

In the second half of the 15th century, the longbow was very frequently used in Burgundian Duke Charles the Bold's armies. During the 1452 siege of Lützelstein (La Petite-Pierre) Castle, Electoral Prince Frederick the Victorious (*Friedrich der Siegreiche*) was wounded in the leg by an arrow, but it is not completely clear whether it could have been a crossbow bolt. The same is the case for the death of the notorious Hans von Rechberg who died in 1464 from an arrow shot by a peasant.

Knights still played a large role, and they were even still important as actors. Individual knights could trigger political landslides with their private deals, think of the Gradner brothers (who as Sigismund's advisors were of considerable influence). But they were gradually marginalized by the growing power of sovereigns. This process was very evident during the reign of Sigismund's father Frederick.

Nobles' castles played a substantial role. If a castle was used as a base for military actions, it became an important piece in the power structure. When brigands or only a simple band of robbers somehow could obtain a castle or when a revengeful or greedy castle lord voluntarily opened the gates, it turned into a real problem, even more so when the castle was topographically advantageous (think of the Beseno Castle).[206] Usually the sovereign's power was adequate to rather quickly capture such a robber's nest. Armies made up of knights had served their purpose, even though many knights did not want to accept it. Strasbourg's victory at Hausbergen in 1262 had already shown that the cities' foot soldiers had a real chance of defeating the nobility's levy of knights. In the 14th century, it was clear that the knightly army's military dominance had ended. That was clearly demonstrated by the Swiss victories and the English successes, based on the longbow, in the Hundred Years War. Nonetheless, the noble cavalry, that is the mounted knights, were still a considerable part of an army. If a political leader, like an imperial prince or a steward, in the described period, did not limit himself to the political-strategic management/control or at least the military-operational command, but he actively took part in the actual fighting as a mounted knight (and here the knightly conventions were in contrast to the military requirements), then his actions were

---

201 Ibid., p. 338.

202 Maximilian first started calling himself the "Elected Roman Emperor" ("*Erwählter Römischer Kaiser*") in 1508, without having made a visit to Rome. He had, however, the concurrence of the Pope (Julius II). The proclamation took place in the Trento Cathedral.

203 The *Feuerrohr* was often also called a "*Stangenbüchse*," literally a "staff gun" or "bar gun."

204 And that already says a lot about the impermeability to gas of these early handheld firearms.

205 See Ortenburg, *Waffen der Landsknechte*, pp. 50–51.

206 Castel Beseno is a mighty fortress occupying the top of a whole hill, in a dominant position over the Adige Valley.

The soldier in the center with the long pike carries a so-called "long knife" *("Langes Messer")* **as a second weapon.**
Photo: Fred Wutz

in the knightly tradition. The later King Maximilian first broke with this tradition in that he fought within the ranks of the foot soldiers at the Battle of Guinegate.

But there were also changes occurring with the cavalry that were not only technical but also tactical in nature. The basic structure of the cavalry was notably stable, in this there was little difference between France, the Holy Roman Empire (north of the Alps) and Burgundy, although there were minor variations.

The tactical unit was the "lance", sometimes also called the "glaive" (German: "*Glefe*"), both the name and the structure still coming from the feudal armies of the high middle ages. In the 15th century, the nucleus and at the same time the military leader of a lance was a knight or a squire. He wore armor and carried a cavalry lance, corresponding to the cliché picture of a medieval knight. Despite that, he in no way had to have already been knighted. He usually carried a hand-and-a-half sword and a shorter sword and falchion (like the "Malchus"). The mace, war hammer, morning star were additional weapons that were effective against armored opponents.

Then there was the lance leader's page, also usually from a knightly family. He was far more than an officer's orderly, because he was simultaneously learning the art of war. And then there was a swordsman (in German called a "*Degenkämpfer*", in France and Burgundy called a "*coutilier*: or *coustillier*"), a youth equipped at the lance leader's expense who also wore armor and was armed with a sword or thrusting rapier and usually employed a polearm (like the ox tongue, the awl pike, etc.).

Plus, there were three mounted bowman, crossbowmen or hand-gunners, and often three more fighters on foot.[207]

It is clear that this formation was not exclusively thought of for cavalry attacks with leveled lances, but rather it was also used in part for infantry and demonstrated a relatively strong defensive capability. This tactical formation was especially widespread in France, Burgundy, and Flanders. Principally, the same was true in the Empire, but there the influence of the knights' orders (that is the "true" barracked knights' units) was evident. Several "lances" formed a "banner", whereby it is not possible to calculate a total of personnel based on the number of "lances" because frequently a "lance" was accompanied by volunteers of diverse (also questionable) quality and numbers. The "*Bannerherr*", who appeared as the commander of a "banner", oddly did not always have to be a knight, the most famous exception was the Breton Bertrand du Guesclin,[208] who as a squire, became a leader of a banner. Several banners formed a division on the battlefield.

In France in 1445, King Charles VII standardized the "full lance" (French "*lance fournie*") as the lance leader (usually a knight), his page, a *coustillier*, two mounted archers or a man-at-arms. Twenty Ordinance Companies were structured on this pattern, each consisting of one hundred "lances". They formed the groundwork of France's new professional army. There were the 'great ordinance companies" (*compagnies de grande ordonnance*) that were preferred, were highly regarded and received higher pay. The "small ordinance companies" (*compagnies de petite ordonnance*) were less well regarded but had the same tactical structure. The French king's mounted ordinance companies proved their worth in the August 1479 Battle of Guinegate.

The Duke of Burgundy copied and further developed the French system. Charles the Bold began the creation of his ordinance companies in 1470. In 1473, a Burgundian ordinance companies was made up of 100 "lances", each with a lance leader, a page, a *coustillier*, three mounted archers and three infantrymen.[209]

In some regions of the Empire, especially in the east, the old feudal army structure existed into the 14th century. The cavalry's elite were sometimes (incorrectly) referred to as "*Renner*" ('runners'), also an indicator that the knight's military function and social status were diverging. The "glaive" (*Glefe*) was normally somewhat smaller than the French "lance". Besides the knight, it had an armored swordsman (*Degenkämpfer*) comparable to the *coustillier*, a light cavalryman or mounted crossbowman and the *Renner*'s page[210]. The system varied greatly. For example, in the Empire a *Glefe* could have up to ten men, but the number was usually less, sometimes only three fighting men (like in the case of Lord Meinhardt "Meinecke" von Schierstädt from Anhalt who provided 100 *Glefen* to Emperor Charles IV in 1373).

The alliances made up of towns throughout the Empire hired elite cavalry units that sometimes called themselves "Squires of Freedom" ("*Knechte der Freiheit*"). The knights' unions (*Ritterbünde*),[211] which were common in southwestern Germany, developed on this model. In Swabia the Sankt Jörgenschild *Ritterbund*, which was founded in reaction to the Appenzell War, was very important. In Tirol, one such union or company, the Elephant Union (*Elefantenbund*) was briefly important at the beginning of the 15th century. After a short military conflict with the Appenzellers who had pushed over the Arlberg as far as Imst in 1405 and then following the hostilities between the brothers Duke Leopold IV and Ernst the Iron (*der Eiserne*), 21 knights in North and South Tirol joined together on

---

207 See Funcken, Fred and Liliane, *Rüstungen und Kriegsgerät im Mittelalter*, p. 88.

208 He rose to be the Constable of France.

209 See Funcken, Fred and Liliane, *Rüstungen und Kriegsgerät der Ritter und Landsknechte*, p. 38.

210 See Nicolle, David, *Medieval Warfare Source Book, Warfare in western Christendom* (London: Arms & Armour, 1999), p. 170.

211 The designation "nobles' companies" (*Adelsgesellschaften*) would be more appropriate and historically accurate, but less recognized.

The strengths of the cavalry lay in its great mobility and the enormous impact power in the attack.
In the attack, the thrusting lance was carried as the primary weapon, as it had been for ages. With the development of plate armor, the shield became superfluous as a means of protection. This Tirolean *Reisiger* has lost his lance during the first charge against the Venetian advance guard. Now he rides back with his drawn sword before his chest to form up again with his detachment.
Photo: Richard J. Kyte

23 August 1406 to form a nobles' company to defend their class' rights against Tirol's sovereign Duke Frederick IV as well as against the Commander of the Land (*Landeshauptmann*) Heinrich VI von Rottenburg. The union remained in existence until 23 March 1407. It was replaced by the "Falcon's Union ("*Falkenbund*"), which existed until 1411. This *Falkenbund*, led by Heinrich VI von Rottenburg of all people, gave the sovereign some problems. Duke Frederick IV, who was opposed to both the Elephant and the Falcon's Unions, acted very cleverly when he himself joined the Union on 24 March 1408.[212] The Tirolean *Ritterbünde* never achieved the military significance like that of the Sankt Jörgenschild union in Swabia.

In the sources, the knights mostly appear as "*milites*" (in Latin), the squires as "*armiger*" (in German), the *Reisigen* often as "*ecuyer*" (French for squire), sometimes also as "*Renner*".

The wealthier burghers of larger town like Speyer, Worms or Strasbourg served as cavalrymen. The nobility; horsemen, (organized in *Glefen*), did not make up an insignificant part of the Imperial towns' forces; frequently hired mercenaries[213] supplemented the cavalry. Since the 14th century at the latest, bands of free men ("*Freischaren*)" played an important role in the military forces in southwestern German territories, for example the "*Blutharste*" in the Alsace and Switzerland. Turning back to the cavalry as a branch, its nucleus was still the armored knight, etc. The armor was mostly of German and Italian models whereby the former allowed its wearer greater mobility with its elaborate overlapping construction than the rigid Italian models. A good, mass-produced set of armor for a 1.6 meter/ 5 foot 3-inch-tall man weighed about 25 kilograms or 55 pounds.[214] A horse is able to carry approximately one quarter of its own weight. For example, at the beginning of the 20th century, a cavalry horse weighed around 450 kilograms or 1,000 pounds. In the German and British cavalry at the beginning of the First World War, the amount of weight that a cavalry mount had to carry was around 125 kilos or 275 pounds or a little more. If one accepts the weight of armor, helmet and weapons as about 30 kilos or 66 pounds, and for the rider and saddle another 80 kilos/175 pounds, then it totals 110 kilos or 242 pounds, and then possibly also the added weight of the horse's armor.[215]

A mounted fighter received a weekly pay of a Rhenish guilder around the beginning of the 15th century; at the start of the 16th century, it was normally two Rhenish guilders, and as a rule, foot soldiers received half that much.

The cavalry was commanded by a marshal. As a rule, that was a hereditary (and very respected) office that was also tied to a not inconsiderable income. At the time in question, the Empire's hereditary marshals were the von Pappenheim Counts. As mentioned, Alexander von Pappenheim was in the Tirolean army's Bavarian contingent. The marshals were responsible for carrying and protecting the great banner, the so-called "*Hauptpanier*".

As part of the feudal system, a prince's vassals were obligated to perform military service. In Tirol at the time in question, the old feudal system was being complemented and replaced by the administration in the service of affiliated judges and stewards.

Associated with taking over a court position at a prince's court was as a rule the obligation to provide that prince with Reisigen, i.e., armored horsemen. Besides the persons who held actual officers at court, the prince's advisors (*Räte*), customs officers (*Mautner*), tollkeepers (*Zöllner*), Treasurers (*Rentmeister*) and forest masters (*Forstmeister*)[216] were responsible for supplying armored horsemen and horses for military service. The so-called 'servants out of the house' ("*Diener von Haus aus*") were also part of the court servants. The prince had contracts with them that required them to provide support in case of emergencies. This practice was primarily occurred in the Bavarian duchies.

The mounted *Degenkämpfer* (swordsmen) previously mentioned, as well as the riders armed with lances, were considered to be *Reisige*. The mounted crossbowmen, and later the hand-gunners, were also considered *Reisige*. One of their primary missions was skirmishing ("*Harzeliren*") before the collision of the heavy cavalry. The expectation was that the mounted crossbowmen could employ their weapons both dismounted and on horseback. Therefore, it was not possible for them to use a spanning mechanism that required the coordinated use of both hands and feet. As a rule, the mounted crossbowmen's crossbows had less tension force (and so shorter range and less penetration power) than the crossbows used by foot soldiers.

At the time of the Venetian War, hardly anyone could imagine the later great importance of Innsbruck's arsenal ("*Innsbrucker Zeughaus*").[217] Maximilian's artillery system with its employment of artillery that decided campaigns and the standardization of calibers was still very much

---

212 The *Falkenbund* had 126 members, the most prominent names of the Tirolean nobility were represented: Wolkenstein, Brandis, Matsch, Starkenberg, Firmian, Schrofenstein, Frundsberg and more.

213 There are preserved documents that contain the modalities of such mercenaries' contracts. For example, a knight (together with three mounted men) in the service of the city of Strasbourg at the them of Emperor Charles IV, received monthly pay of 30 Rhenish guilders. See Ortenburg, *Waffen der Landsknechte*, p. 21.

214 See Funcken, Fred and Liliane, *Rüstungen und Kriegsgerät im Mittelalter* (Munich: Mosaik,1979), p. 138. A so-called "*Schaller*" (sallet) helmet often was part of the gothic armor.

215 See Embleton, Gerry u. Howe, John, *Söldnerleben im Mittelalter*, Stuttgart: Motorbuch 1996, p. 41.

216 Earlier, the people were often referred to a a group as "*Hofgesinde*" - 'court servants' .

217 In 1503 the Arsenal housed about 150 cannons.

in the future. But in the older descriptions of the Venetian War, almost unanimously spoke about the Tiroleans' artillery superiority. In Tirol the foundation for producing artillery began at the start of the 15th century. The country's riches in wood, use of water power, mining of copper and silver were the best prerequisites for such production.[218] Artillery was also produced in the (economically highly developed) Outlands. Firearms that could not be served by just one man were considered artillery.[219] Just in the 16th and 15th centuries handheld firearms and artillery pieces were developed in different directions with respect to their calibers, barrel lengths and weights. In the 15th century there were still many very large handheld firearms that actually have to be counted as artillery. For example, the "*crapadeaux*" were small cannons that were widely used in France and Burgundy at the time.[220] Actually the already obsolete "*couleuvrines*", which were crewed by two men and either mounted on forked supports or wagons, were still present in large numbers. These *couleuvrines* represented a bigger version of firearms referred to as *couleuvrines a main*.

In Burgundian Duke Charles' arsenal there had been many of these kinds of cannons of questionable effectiveness and many had gotten into the hands of his adversaries as booty. Realistically oriented commanders like Kappler and Sanseverino recognized the usefulness (or non-usefulness) of obsolete ordinance, but antiquated firearms were common in castles and the towns' arsenals. Possession of large artillery pieces was so very much a question of prestige, that they were maintained long beyond their real time.[221]

It is said that a cannon, which definitively came from an arsenal in the Habsburg Outlands, was used in the Burgundian Wars. It was the "Kätherlien" ("Cathy") from Alsatian town of Ensisheim, that played a role at the siege of Blamont.

The field artillery had made great advances in the 15th century. Although this period of experimentation produced unmanageable numbers of cannon types, a certain (but not complete) standardization first occurred in the Burgundian Wars. Burgundy was leading in artillery, and from Charles the Bold's defeats, so many cannons fell into the hands of the Swiss, Lorrainers, the Alsatians and the Tiroleans as booty, that the Burgundian kinds could be considered the standards. The most widespread kinds included the Serpentines with a caliber from 50mm to 150mm and the *Veuglaires* with a caliber from 50mm to 250mm. Frequently the cannons were produced as

Field gun in position, in this case a breech-loader for which the tankard-like loading chamber is attached behind the gun's barrel.
Photo: Anja Hiebinger

---

218 See Fiedler, *Taktik und Strategie der Landsknechte*, p. 130.

219 See Ortenburg, *Waffen der Landsknechte*, pp. 63–64.

220 See Smith, Robert Douglas and DeVries, Kelly, *Medieval Weapons: An Illustrated History of Their Impact* (Santa Barbara: ABC-CLIO, 2007), p. 294.

221 See Turnbull, Stephen, *The Art of Renaissance Warfare, From the Fall of Constantinople to the Thirty Years War* (Barnsley: Greenhill Books, 2006), p. 42.

breechloaders having a loading chamber (that looked like a beer tankard) that was fastened behind the barrel. That permitted the cannon to fire two to three times per minute, but when it fired, a large portion of the gas pressure was lost.[222] Field artillery was produced using a stave-band process (described further below) or bronze casting. Cannons from the Burgundian booty are preserved in the La Neuveville Museum in Switzerland. A wrought-iron serpentine field gun with a total length of 3.6 meters or 11 feet 10 inches had a 1.58 meter or 5 foot 2-inch-long barrel and a 75 millimeter or 3-inch caliber. It was one of the Serpentines.[223] The *"Tarrasbüchsen"* or 'trestle guns' so often mentioned in the accounts are difficult to classify.

The traditional bronze casting method could not suffice for the larger cannons because the relatively large powder changes built up too great pressure in the barrel, which could lead to the bursting of the barrel. Therefore, the large (siege) cannons (also called "bombards"[224]) were produced as so-called stave-band cannon (German *"Stabringgeschütze"*). These kinds of cannons were made of rectangular or trapezoidal iron staves (of high-quality materials) laid down in a circle and bundled with red-hot iron bands that held the iron staves in place when the bands cooled. The smith produced a wood core for the bore around which the staves were arranged radially and the bands were placed around the staves (not unlike how bands are put on wooden barrels). In the 15th century a series of large caliber stave-band cannon were produced: the *"Faule Magd"* ("Lazy Maiden" – preserved in the Dresden Military Museum), the *"Dulle Griet"* (preserved in Ghent), and Mons Meg (located at Edinburgh Castle). The bronze casting process had, however, made considerable advances in the last decades before the Venetian War.

The cannons *"Faule Mette"* ("Lazy Mette") of Braunschweig and *"Faule Grete"* ("Lazy Gretel") of Marienburg, produced using the bronze casing method, were much larger than the iron stave-band cannons (but unfortunately no longer preserved). These bombards, in so far as they were made with the stave-band process, fired along with "hail" (*"Hagel"*, i.e., scrap metal), exclusively stone balls because the gas pressure that occurred with iron cannonballs inevitably burst the barrels. The large siege guns were almost exclusively ones placed on platforms to fire, that is they were transported on special wagons, and firing was done on a firm timber framework or something similar.

Smaller cannons were also already produced using the cast iron process.

The cannons naturally also had corresponding ammunition. In the period in question, in this region the field and siege artillery almost without exception fired sandstone balls. Elm wood shims were used to pack the pow-

---

222 Embleton and Howe, *Söldnerleben im Mittelalter*, pp. 70–71.

223 See Reid, William, *Buch der Waffen, Von der Steinzeit bis zur Gegenwart* (Düsseldorf and Vienna: Econ, 1976), p. 79.

224 Such cannon were produced starting in 1370.

Three artillerymen discuss the positioning of their gun and draw a provisional sketch on the ground.
The fieldpiece standing next to them is a so-called "breechloader" that has powder chambers that can be exchanged.
With it, a practiced crew can maintain continuous firing of balls or shrapnel in rapid succession.
Photo: Condottieri Mauriziani

der charge against the stone projectiles. In contrast to the handheld firearms, the artillery was already using granulated gunpowder, but very finely ground powder" ("*Mehlpulver*") was used for the igniting charge. In Strasbourg in the 1470s, linden trees were specially planted in the open spaces just inside the city walls in order to obtain charcoal (for producing gunpowder).[225]

Cannons still had not actually completely replaced catapults and trebuchets.

At the 1448 siege of the Wasselnheim Castle in Alsace by Strasbourg forces, they threw feces ("*Ulmer Grün*") into the castle with a catapult.[226] In 1504, the Kurpfalz forces still used a trebuchet at the siege of the Altwolfstein Castle.

Draft animals, often in great numbers, were needed to move larger artillery pieces, whether cannons or catapults. They could be strong horse breeds (not dissimilar to our present-day cold bloods) or oxen. An army in the late 15th century would be accompanied by a considerable baggage train that required many draft animals and some specialists (craftsmen). At the siege of the Tannenberg (an der Bergstrasse) Castle in June-July 1399, 20 horses were needed to move the "*Frankfurter Geschütz*" (Frankfurt Cannon), a stone projectile-firing cannon. For 21 days, this monstrous cannon bombarded the castle with stone balls until it had opened a breech in the almost 3-meter thick curtain wall. To do it used almost 400 kilograms (880 pounds) of black powder.[227]

Back to the baggage train: around the middle of the 15th century, an army was accompanied by many wagons, of which a large portion transported provisions. There were also wagons that specifically served for defense in a wagon fort (*Wagenburg* or laager), and combination supply and war wagons. The latter had been widely adopted in the German-speaking regions based on the impression they made in the Hussite Wars. Two handbooks give information about the configuration of such wagons, the first is from the time of the Hussite Wars (so about 1425) and the second is by Margrave Albrecht Achilles of Brandenburg (around 1460).[228] In the first work, a war wagon ("*Kriegswagen*"), among other things, is described thusly: It should be pulled by five horse teams and have a crew of 21 (!) men. They included five riders (with armor) for the draft horses, four hand-gunners, four crossbowmen, and specialists like a smith, a wagon-maker etc. Five such wagons formed a "member' ("*Glied*"), and five "members" ("*Glieder*") formed a "union" ("*Bund*"), and four "unions" ("*Bünde*") formed a "*Schickung*" (i.e., one hundred war wagons). Each "*Schickung*" also had 100 supply wagons for provisions ("*Speiswagen*"). A well defended *Wagenburg* (laager) could be set up using chains and short palisades that were carried in the war wagons. Some of the wagons brought along small caliber cannons, some mounted on rotatable trunnion limbers,[229] so a *Wagenburg* could have considerable defensive capability.

---

225 Krieg von Hochfelden, Georg Heinrich, *Geschichte der Militär-Architektur in Deutschland* (Stuttgart: Ebner & Seubert 1859), p. 270.

226 "*Meister Graßeck warf mit seiner Schleudermaschine hundertneunundachzig Mal Koth und Steine ins Schloß.*" ("Master Gasseck hurled dung and stones into the castle one hundred eighty-nine times with his catapult.") Strobel, Adam Walther, *Vaterländische Geschichte des Elsasses*, p. 228.

227 See Lachmann et al., *eyn rohr aus eisern stangen, Zur Geschichte des Stabringgeschützes „Faule Magd"* (Dresden: no year), p. 18.

228 See Würdinger, *Kriegsgeschichte*, II. Band, pp. 378–379.

229 Similar to the swivel guns on warships.

Horseman in plate armor ▶
Photo: Condottieri Mauriziani

The Venetian Forces

At the time of these events, the Venetian Republic's territories outside of Italy were larger than the Italian lands. The Venice's military forces for maintaining its maritime and land empire outside Italy (for example in the center of the eastern Mediterranean) were structured differently than those employed against the Italian neighbors. The latter differed little from those of the other Italian states.

As Venice became a major power in the course of the 14th century, a "lance" consisting of the horseman, two pages and three lightly armed riders evolved (like elsewhere in Italy). The necessity to fight in Greece, on the Dalmatian Coast and elsewhere, led to abandoning an old law whereby a Venetian nobleman was not allowed to command more than 25 armed followers.[230] This law originated in the 12th century and could have been based on a concern about armed factional fighting within the city.

The governors of the colonies had units whose numbers were strictly established. Such a *bandiera* was commanded by a *comestabilis* and had more than 20 foot soldiers and 15 to 18 cavalrymen. In addition, in the case of the most important colony, Crete, the residents in the north of this Venetian feudal property could be called up for military service. The Greek *Sfakiotes* lived in the island's impassible south and were largely left to their own devices. When they were not in open rebellion, the *Sfakiotes* could be hired as mercenaries. They were very skilled archers on foot.[231]

It took a very long time until the Venetians viewed the Ottomans as their primary enemy. That is the only way it is explainable that the republic on the Lagoon enmeshed itself in so many inner-Italian conflicts.

After an attempted revolt in 1310 and the subsequent creation of the "Council of Ten", Venice established a small standing unit of 630 soldiers for defense of the Republic. One hundred patrolled the Lagoon in small boats, 30 guarded the Doge's palace and 200[232] protected St. Mark's Square. Each ten were responsible for the security of a community district (*contrada*) of which there were thirty.

The weapons and armor of the majority of these troops were stored in the palace's arsenal; the Council of Ten was responsible for the weapons and therefore they bore the 'CX" inscription. The Council of Ten was also responsible for the Venetians' very capable espionage network.[233]

Additionally, each city quarter maintained a 1,500-man militia for emergencies. In such circumstances, half of the men were to report to St. Mark's Square and the other half were to protect their own district. Venice had numerically the largest city militia of all the Italian states; a census in 1356 reported that the city could count 40,100 able-bodied men between the ages of 20 and 60. The militia was organized in groups of twelve men (*duodene*). One man from among them was chosen by lottery for active duty, but the others bore the financial costs. Should the need arise, a second man, and if necessary a third man could be chosen by lottery. Sometimes three men were chosen by lottery from the start, for example in the wars against Genoa in 1350 and 1278. The duration of service was set by the Council of Ten; there were examples in which it was an entire year before the man could return home. This organization form for the city militia existed until the end of the 15th century. Many of its members were taken into the ranks of the *provisionati*, professional mercenary infantry. The militia of Venice's mainland possessions (*terraferma*) formed the short-time existing *provisionati di San Marco*. Each of the *terraferma*'s larger towns and cities was to supply 500 men, e.g., in 1477, between 15,000 and 20,000 men were assembled. When these militia accompanied the Venetian army (usually consisting of mercenaries), they were frequently put to work constructing defenses. In the period up to 1440, the militia was used to form small groups of crossbowmen, usually from 100 to 300 men strong and sometimes up to 800 men. These crossbowmen were organized into troops of 25 men, each commanded by a nobleman.[234] Crossbow shooting was very popular in Venice,[235] later archers also replaced the crossbowmen. Oriental reflex bows were used. The *cinquedea*, (also "*cinqueda*"; in German "*Ochsenzunge*"; in English the ox tongue), a late Middle Ages edged weapon with an extra wide blade, was also popular

---

230 See Nicolle, David, *Medieval Warfare Source Book; Warfare in Western Christendom* (London: Arms & Armour, 1999), p. 173.

231 Ibid. p. 173.

232 They were selected by the Quarter Masters of each of the city's six quarters (*sestieri*).

233 See Heath, Ian, *Armies of the Middle Ages, Volume 2 (The Ottoman Empire, Eastern Europe and the Near East, 1300–1500)* (Worthing: Wargames Research Group, 1984), p. 31.

234 Ibid., p. 31.

235 In 1314 there were 1,131 crossbows stored in the arsenal. The *Compagni della Calza*, founded in the 15th century, was a popular shooting guild. See also Nicolle, David and Rothero, Christopher, *The Venetian Empire 1200–1670* (Oxford: Osprey, 2004), p. 9.

The illustration shows two soldiers with armor ▶ well suited for rapid attack, for example to take a town in a surprise attack. Both are wearing only a little armor. Their elaborately painted shields, so-called *tartsche*s or pavises, show the Lion of St. Mark, the symbol of the Venetian Republic. Together with their swords, they can be used well for fighting in narrow streets.
Photo: Città del Grifo

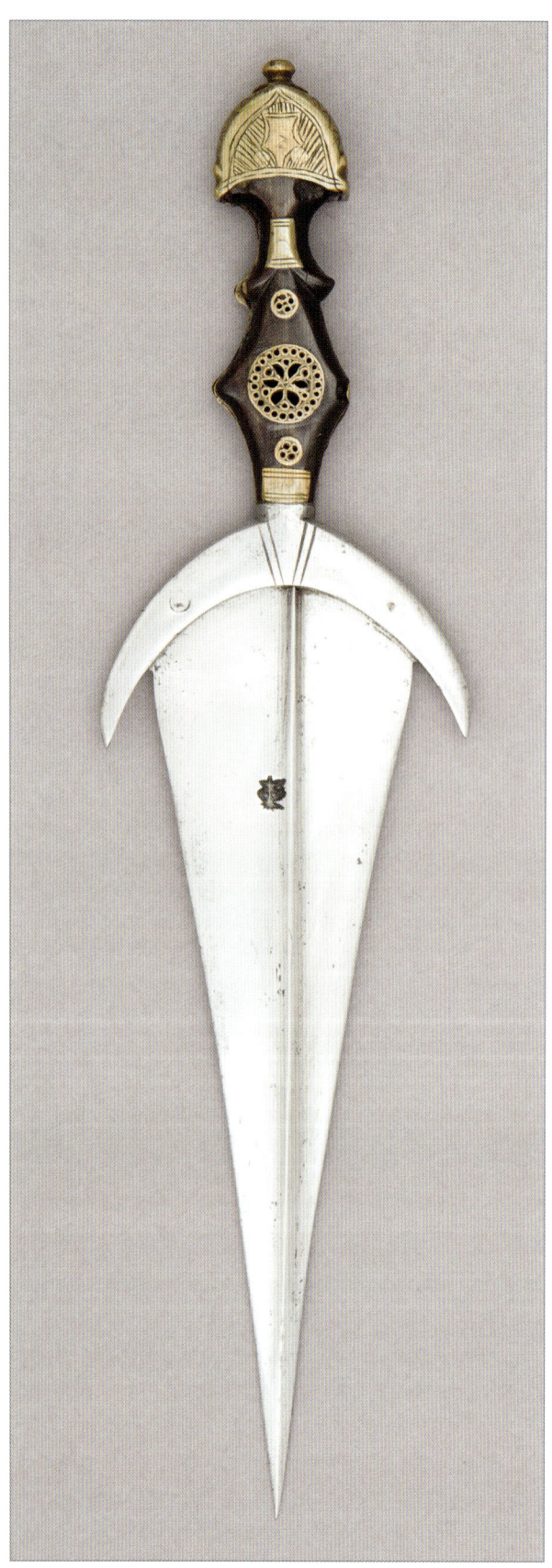

A *cinquedea* (ca. 1500),
Photo: Metropolitan Museum of Art
CC0 1.0 Universal (CC0 1.0)
Public Domain Dedication

with the militiamen. It was developed in Northern Italy and had a total length between 35 and 50 centimeters (about 14 to 20 inches).[236]

In the 14th century, apart from this militia, Venice possessed fewer and fewer ground forces. The Republic relied on its allies and mercenaries. In 1404, Venice hired an army of 9,000 cavalrymen and 10,000 foot soldiers. An initial attempt to create a standing cavalry unit (250 men in 1402) was only short-lived. In 1406 the Senate approved the creation of a permanent unit of 500 "lances"[237] (and some infantrymen). Taddeo dal Verme was named their captain general; he brought along a force of 100 "lances" and 100 foot soldiers. After a campaign against Hungary in 1413, 800 to 900 "lances" were taken into permanent service, in 1422 their number had shrunk to 400, and in 1426 climbed to 3,000.

The Venetian Armies of this period numbered from 20,000 to 30,000 men, two thirds of whom were normally *condottieri*. For example, in 1432 an army had 12,000 hired cavalrymen, 9,000 hired infantrymen, and 11,000 city militiamen. It is evident that after each campaign, Venice retained a growing portion of the hired troops in permanent service, while the rest of the army was released. For example, in 1433 there were 5,000 hired horsemen and 2,000 foot soldiers, in 1454 it was 6,000 horsemen and 2,000 foot soldiers, in 1480[238] 6,000 cavalrymen and 3,000 foot soldiers, and in 1485 there were 6,500 to 7,000 horsemen.

---

236 See Oakeshott, Ewart, *The Sword in the Age of Chivalry* (Woodbridge: Praeger, 1964), p. 78.

237 In Venice, a "lance" consisted of three horsemen until the middle of the 15th century.

238 That was a year when there were already 8,000 horsemen temporarily under contract.

Along with the conventional horn bows ▶ for crossbows, in the 15th century, steel bows were also no longer a rarity. This crossbowman wears a quilted jacket made of many layers of think linen – a good and inexpensive alternative to metal body armor. His helmet is covered with cloth that on one hand fulfills a decorative purpose, and on the other hand prevents a too rapid heating up of the metal by the sun.
Photo: Condottieri Mauriziani

A very popular polearm for the Italian infantry was the *roncone*, a special form of the glaive or billhook.
It usually had a long, slender point in combination with a sharp upward curved hook. For head protection, open helmets like 'iron hats' or hemispherical helmets (*cervelliere*) were especially popular because they did not limit vision or breathing. The foot soldier in the middle wears a salet/salade ("*Schaller*") with an upturned visor, like those also used by the cavalry.
Photo: Città del Grifo

In the first half of the 15th century, a large part of the standing cavalry force consisted of "*lanze spezzate*", horsemen from special units who after their *condottieri's* death or departure from service were taken over into the Republic's permanent service.[239] In 1420 there were 400 *lanze spezzate*, and in 1470 considerably more. From this point in time they were frequently commanded by Venetians, but then from the beginning of the 16th century, they almost completely disappeared.

A quick look at the *condottieri* as a phenomenon is useful at this point.[240]

The term "*condottiere*", plural "condottieri", comes from the Italian and designates the leader of a military unit in the Late Middle Ages. This mercenary leader raised a company of fighters ("*compagnia di ventura*") at his own expense, equipped it with weapons and armor and took care of its training. Then he offered this complete package of an effective military unit to numerous Italian city states that were always in need of soldiers. The details of the agreement were written down in a contract "*condotta*"[241] and hence the name "*condottiere*". Until the middle of the 15th century, it was seldom that a condottiere, when the period of his contract expired, would enter a new one with that same employer, but after 1450, this practice became more frequent. It was not uncommon that a "*condotta di aspetto*" was concluded in which the *condottiere* obtained one third or one half of the money that he kept ready for his fighters for wartime service. If he had to actually go to battle, he received the rest of the money. Most of the time the *condottieri* received an advance on their pay (*imprestanze*). When a *condottiere* entered into a contract with an Italian city state of principality, there was normally already a hired unit. Often the *condottiere* himself had taken subordinate condottieri into his service along with their men based on similar pay contracts. As an example, in 1441, Micheletto Attendolo[242] entered Venetian service, with his cavalry unit of 561 lances, which included 167 subordinated *condottieri*. Their units were between one and 50 *lances* strong.[243] *Condottieri* supposedly also put a lot of value on a certain degree of uniformity. For example, it was quite common that about one

---

239 For example, that is what happened with the companies that had been commanded by Roberto da Montalbodo, Gattamelatta and Bartolomeo Colleoni.
In 1476 there were the *lanza spezzata* of the long since deceased Antonello da Corneto. After the horsemen were taken into Venice's service again, they fought as a standing cavalry unit under a Venetian commander. See Heath: *Armies of the Middle Ages*, Volume 1, p. 35.

240 See also Nicolle, David and Embleton G. A., *Italian Medieval Armies 1300–1500* (London: Osprey, 1983).

241 The term "*condotta*" initially meant "conduct" and only later morphed to mean the document.

242 Micheletto Attendolo, also called Michelotto da Cotignola, (ca. 1390–1451) became the commander in chief of all of Venice's forces in 1441.

243 See Heath, *Armies of the Middle Ages*, Volume 1, p. 36.

third of the *imprestanza* was paid in the form of cloth.[244] By doing so, the *condottieri* could dress their men relatively uniformly.

The armor of the Venetian cavalrymen, who were usually hired, was like that of the other Northern Italian cavalry. Because Venice could afford to hire well-known *condottieri*, their personnel were normally well equipped. The *condottieri* themselves had armor that met the highest military (and frequently also artistic) requirements. For example, Roberto da Sanseverino wore armor at Calliano that came from the workshop of the Milanese armorer Antonio da Missaglia and was made around 1480.[245]

In Italy flexible or also rigid armor made of leather was widespread. Also, an Italian specialty was the "Venetian *salade*" (or *Schaller*) helmet, but which were mostly produced in Milan. Otherwise the barbute (Italian "*barbuta*") – another kind of helmet was especially popular.

Large units of hired cavalry were divided into squadrons (*squadre*), of which the largest was normally the *condottiere*'s *casa* (i.e., the household). Also, bodyguards, administrative personnel, etc. were located there. The other squadrons were commanded by *caposquadre* or *squadrieri*. The size of a *squadra* was not fixed.

The smallest tactical unit (if one wants to use the modern term) was the "*lance*". In Venice, like in the rest of Italy, a *lance* consisted of three men: a heavily armored fighter armed with a lance, a somewhat more lightly armored horseman and a mounted servant or page. The lance leader (usually a knight) was called an *elmetto* or *vero armigero*. Around 1470 the lance already included four horsemen, even though this form of organization was only first recognized in peacetime starting in 1490. The additional man was almost always a mounted crossbowman. Around 1490 the group of mounted crossbowmen had grown. They constituted a corps with the cavalry and were under their own commander. A third of the cavalry consisted of mounted crossbowmen, another third of *elmetti*, and the last third of light cavalry. Frequently the mounted crossbowmen also served as a condottiere's body guard. There were also a growing number of mounted hand-gunners.

The Italian *lances*, unlike those in France or Burgundy, did not include foot soldiers.

At the start they were still divided into spearmen, crossbowmen and shield-bearers. Later (around 1440), the was a dividing into, on one hand hand gunners, archers and crossbowmen and on the other hand pikemen, halberdiers, swordsmen and buckler shield-bearers. Regular hand-gunner companies were introduced between 1435 and 1448, whereby the gunners mostly came from regions north of the Alps. Firearms training for Venice's citizens, which was intended to reduce the dependence

A well-armored Venetian ensign with a barbuta helmet and plate armor.
He is surrounded by the men of his color guard, which in contrast to the men in the background, are armed with battle axes or war hammers. These are shorter than the polearms of the other personnel and can be more easily used in close combat around the flag. But they are long enough to deliver a powerful blow with both hands.
Photo: Città del Grifo

---

244 See ibid. p. 126.
245 See Wagner, E., Drobna, Z. und Durdik, J., *Medieval Costume, Armour and Weapons* (London: Andrew Dakers, 1962), p. 66.

The armor of important personalities like commanders, princes and kings was often not only of the highest functional quality, but also occasionally lavishly decorated. Gilding, painting and coverings of the finest textiles announced the wearer's nearly superhuman social status.
Photo: Condottieri Mauriziani

on foreign hand-gunner companies, first started around 1490.[246] In addition, there were Swiss mercenary units and Albanian and Cretan foot soldiers.

Venice's armies were led by well-known condottieri; the rich city on the Lagoon could afford the most prominent and most expensive ones: Gonzaga, Attendolo, Carmagnola, Colleoni.

Nevertheless, on campaigns Venice's hired armies were always accompanied by one or two high-ranking Venetian noblemen, so-called "*provveditori*". They were to ensure that the Republic's interests were always safeguarded. At times they also took over command of individual troop units.

In the course of its campaigns in Morea (in the Peloponnesus) and Dalmatia, the Venetians came in contact with the so-called "Stradiots" (or "stradioti"), who they quickly took into their service. The Stradiots showed themselves to be more effective than Italian style cavalry against the Ottomans. They were used for the first time in Venetian service in great numbers in the war from 1463 to 1479 against the Ottomans. One of the Stradiots'

first leaders in Venetian service as Konstantinos Graitzas Palaiologos.[247] These Stradiots were also employed by Venice in the Friuli region at the end of the 1470s, then also on the Italian peninsula. In 1479, 1,000 of them were permanently taken into service and brought to Italy, plus another 1,000 in 1482. Because they proved to be effective in the 1482 war against Ferrara, other Italian principalities followed Venice's example. For example, Naples took them into its service, but they were also in Milan's service.[248] In their role as light cavalry, the Stradiots wore a mixture of oriental and Byzantine clothing, a cape and a small hat,[249] or a light helmet. They were armed with lances, oriental style bows and arrows, scimitars, and with maces. Pointed hats appear to have been characteristic for them. The Stradiots crop up very frequently in the Fri-

---

246 In 1493, the Friuli region was already able to raise a militia unit of 900 hand-gunners.

247 He was actually distantly related with Byzantium's last ruling house.

248 The Stradiots, often Albanians, were feared. Allegedly their pay was a bounty: one Venetian ducat per head. According to a legend, at the Battle of Fornovo a Stradiot, who was supposed to receive a bounty for the head of a Frenchman did not find one. Therefore he improvised by attacking and beheading an Italian priest.

249 Therefore – because of their hats – the Stradiots were also called "*cappelletti*" ("little hats") in Venice.

uli region. Venice had other exotic units but they played no role in the Italian or Alpine theaters of war.[250] Venice was also one of the states that employed Swiss mercenaries. In the first half of the 15th century there were already men from the Swiss Confederation and Graubunden[251] in Venice's wartime service who had been recruited without treaties between the Republic and the respective Swiss *Orte*. In this connection, the first Venetian emissaries appeared on Swiss soil, for example in 1425, Giovanni Amati in Lucerne, as well as Francesco Brunicardi in 1439 and finally Niccolò Bernardo in Zurich in 1463. The latter attempted to conclude a military alliance which the Confederates rejected just like they did to a petition to recruit 1,000 mercenaries in 1478.

The Lion of St. Mark decorates this soldier's pavis as a heraldic symbol.
Photo: Città del Grifo

A Stradiot, handbill from 1529

---

250 However the "*getarii*" should be mentioned here. It was a mercenary group with a bad reputation that was present in Salonika, which belonged to the Venetian empire from 1423 to 1430. The city was under Ottoman siege the whole tie and the *getarii* were supposed to mingle with the residents and militiamen and kill anyone who carelessly expressed the willingness to capitulate.

251 At that time, there were very few merchants and craftsmen from the Swiss Confederation in Venice, but large numbers from Graubunden.

This pavis is also decorated with the Lion of St. Mark.
Photo: Città del Grifo

When, from 1482 to 1484, the Venetians fought against the Duke of Ferrara, Ercole I d´Este, in the so-called *"Guerra del Sale"* (Salt War), they also hired Swiss mercenaries whose effectiveness was renowned. They were able to hire a considerable number of *Reislaufer*s and especially many Bernese, whose captain Peter Keyser was from Bern. Additionally, they hired 300 men from Appenzell and the Rhine Valley under Captain Schöni von Appenzell. In 1482 the mercenaries, led by Duke René (Renatus) II of Lorraine, went into Italy. In November 1482 the Venetians under Roberto da Sanseverino, had almost defeated Ferrara, when their former ally, Pope Sixtus IV, quit the alliance. Because the Confederation had a treaty with Pope Sixtus IV at that time, they were urged to return home very shortly after setting out. In the meantime, it seems that this papal order was not followed in full, so for example, the Appenzellers were employed under the Venetian commander, Sanseverino, in the fighting in the Polesina region.[252]

The Venetian Republic also sought Tiroleans as mercenaries. For example, in 1482 the Doge sent a letter to Archduke Sigismund asking if they could not recruit mercenaries in Tirol in exchange for grain deliveries.[253]

The Venetians artillery was noteworthy. Their world-famous arsenal was not only a storage area, but also a production site for many cannons.

Venice already had cannons in the first half of the 14th Century, and in 1379 they began to equip their warships with them. When Arnold von Harff[254] visited the Venetian city's arsenal in 1497, according to his account it contained three mortars, 30 major cannons, 160 large cannons, 44 siege guns ("*Kartaunen*") and more than 500 smaller cannons. Almost all were of copper-bronze, that is produced by casting. There were giant bombards in the artillery park that could fire very heavy balls. More important was that 400 of the smaller cannons had wheeled carriages, i.e., they were suited for land warfare. [255] Harff remarked that he had never seen such a large number of cannons, although he had also visited the arsenals in Brescia, Verona, Padua and Vienna. He was told that the Venetian possessions' arsenals held even more cannons. In 1471 Venice began to instruct large numbers of Venetians on how to produce and operate cannons. However, around the end of the 15th century, the majority of artillerymen were Burgundians, Englishmen and Germans. The arsenal was a first-class production center, producing cannons, but also bowstrings for crossbows.

---

252 See Rudolph, *Kriegsgeschichte der Schweizer*, p. 225.

253 The letter dated from 4 March 1482.

254 Arnold von Harff (born in 1471 in the Castle Harff bei Bedburg, died there in January 1505) was a knight who visited medieval Christianity's three most important pilgrimage sites, namely Rome, Jerusalem and Santiago de Compostela, and who wrote a comprehensive report in German about his travels.

255 See Heath, *Armies of the Middle Ages, Volume 2*, p. 33.

The Sonnenburg Benedictine Nunnery
Illustration: Wolfgang Braun

Armor and edged weapons were primarily manufactured in Brescia,[256] which was part of Venice's territories starting the first half of the 15th century.[257]

The nucleus of Venetian military power was always the Republic's fleet. But naturally it did not play a special role in this conflict's theater. However, the fleet's crews were a large reservoir for militarily capable personnel. Additionally, a society that was based on maritime trade naturally had useful expertise that was helpful for river crossings. But the Venetians' nautical experience also provided other militarily useful capabilities.[258]

Venetian fleet definitely carried out operations on Lake Garda and on the lower stretches of the Po River. Its small boats (*barche*) that had a crew of five men, two of whom functioned as crossbowmen, were not its only contributions.

In the winter of 1438-1439 Venetian forces under the leadership of Nicolò Sorbolo, a Venetian militia officer from Candia (on Crete), brought six full-sized galleys and 25 smaller ships up the Adige River, and then transported them overland through partially difficult terrain to Lake Garda.[259] To do so took 2,000 draft animals. The ships were to help relieve the Venetian garrison in Brescia that was besieged by the Milanese. On their 20-kilometer (12.4 mile) route, the fleet had to conquer the San Giovanni Pass (287 meters/942 feet above sea level) and get through the Santa Lucia Valley's narrow gorge. On the steep descent to Torbole on Lake Garda (68 meter/233 foot elevation) they had to use the sails of heavy ships as brakes. However, this fleet was destroyed by a Milanese flotilla at the battle at Maderno on 26 September.[260] Consequently the Venetians never brought another fleet to Lake Garda using this method, but afterward transported ready-made ship components and assembled them in Torbole. In April 1440 the Venetian flotilla, newly consisting of many galleys and smaller boats, devastated the Milanese fleet before Riva del Garda. So not only did the Venetians succeed in the desired relief of Brescia, but they were able to bring all of Lake Garda under Venice's control[261].

---

256 See Nicolle and Rothero, *The Venetian Empire 1200–1670*, pp. 41 - 42.

257 Venice had conquered the city in 1426. See Lühe, Hanns Eggert Willibald von der (Hg.): *Militair-Conversations-Lexicon* (Leipzig: C. Brüggemann, 1833), p. 703.

258 Naturally navigating by the stars, water storage, and logistical calculations were also useful on land.

259 In Venice, they later called the adventure "*Galeas per montes*". The daring undertaking was artistically imortalized by Tintoretto on the ceiling of the chamber of the Great Council in Venice. t

260 See Nicolle and Rothero, *The Venetian Empire*, p. 9.

261 See also Heller, Ferdinand (trans.), *Das glorreiche Unterfangen. Galeeren auf Bergfahrt zum Gardasee; Erzählung in zwanzig Bildern* (Trento: Curcu & Genovese, 2015).

Weapons practice by Italian foot soldiers, Photo: Città del Grifo

THE BATTLE IN THE ENNE MOUNTAINS

Until 1447, Nikolaus von Kues was traveling throughout the Roman Empire as the legate in the service of Pope Eugene IV and represented his interests at imperial meetings. In this role, he rather certainly intervened for the Pope, which impressed contemporaries and posterity. One hundred years later Johannes Kymeus, a devout Protestant, joked in a handbill that Cusanus was "the Pope's Hercules against the Germans." [262]

Cusanus wanted to reform the Empires monastic landscape in order to strengthen the Church's role. Many monasteries had strayed from the teachings of St. Benedict and behaved in a thoroughly worldly manner. In this sense, he also supported the so-called "Congregation of Bursfeld Abbey ("*Bursfelder Kongregation*"), a union of western and central German monasteries. They were committed to a return to the original rules of monasticism. In 1451, Cusanus confirmed the unification of the congregation.

In 1448, Pope Nicolas V named Cusanus officially to be a cardinal and in 1450 also the Prince-Bishop of Brixen. This appointment took place bypassing the Cathedral Chapter (*Domkapitel*), which had the right to vote on it, and without consultation with Tirol's sovereign, Sigismund. His own candidate, Leonhard Wismeyer, had been deposed beforehand by the Pope. In his time as the Bishop of Brixen, Cusanus was repeatedly in conflict with the Tirolean sovereign. At the peak of this conflict, Duke Sigismund besieged the Bishop in the town of Bruneck in 1460. After a bloodless agreement, Cusanus was captured and had to give up many of his reforming ideas.

With the appointment of the reform-oriented Cusanus to be the Bishop of Brixen, new times dawned in the Brixen Diocese. Cusanus tried to get back the powers that the Bishops had ceded to their stewards, the Count of Tirol and Görz in the course of the Late Middle Ages. A first step was centralizing episcopal power. Yet many monasteries among others, which could invoke centuries-long self-administration, stood in his way. [263]

---

262 Quoted as "*Des Babsts Hercules wider die Deudschen*" Kremer, Klaus, *Nikolaus von Kues (1401-1464), Einer der größten Deutschen des 15. Jahrhunderts* (Trier: Paulinus, 1999), p. 22.

263 Hallauer, Hermann,:*Die Schlacht im Enneberg, Neue Quellen zur moralischen Wertung des Nikolaus von Kues* (Trier: Kleine Schriften der. Cusanus-Gesellschaft, 1969), p. 5.

One of these institutions was the Sonnenburg Benedictine monastery in the Puster Valley (*Pustertal*). Thanks to numerous endowments it possessed extensive lands in the Gader Valley (*Gadertal*), where it exercised lower court jurisdiction. The higher court jurisdiction in this region was in contrast carried out by the Bishop of Brixen, so that inevitably frictions arose. A third component was added to this conflict, namely the Tirolean sovereign. Duke Sigismund claimed to have the rights as a Steward (*Vogteirechte*) for the valley because he was officially the patron of the Sonnenburg nuns.

When Cusanus tried to carry out the reform of the man worldly monastic communities in the diocese, he encountered stiff resistance at Sonnenburg. The Abbess Verena von Stuben maligned the Bishop by claiming that he was actually going after the monastery's worldly possessions. Because she refused to obey Cusanus, the Bishop excommunicated the Abbess and put the cloister under an interdict. Verena von Stuben appeared to be less than impressed because she was supported by Duke Sigismund. He had taken over the armed protection of the cloister and through his administrator, the knight Balthasar von Welsberg carried out a number of pinpricks against the Bishop's subjects. Bishop Cusanus did not want to give up his rights but could not afford to wage open warfare against the sovereign.

Nicolaus Cusanus interpreted these actions by Welsberg as a personal insult. The Bishop no longer felt secure enough in Brixen and because he feared for his life, he fled to the Buchenstein Castle (now *Castel Andraz*). This fortification lay in the most southeasterly part of Brixen's domain and to this day still seems defensible.

Despite mediation by Duchess Eleonore, Sigismund's wife, no agreement could be reached. When Duke Sigismund left Tirol for a short time, Balthasar von Welsburg resigned his office as the cloister's administrator and protector. Verena von Stuben then had to worry about its security. She tasked her brother-in-law, Jobst von Hornstein zu Schatzberg, to hire a unit of mercenaries. She wanted to use them to force the abbey's tenants in the Gader Valley to pay their taxes only to the cloister and no longer to the Bishop of Brixen.[264]

On the evening of 5 April 1458 Jobst von Hornstein departed on his mission with 86 men. In the morning hours the troops finally reached the principal town, Enneberg, where they immediately forcefully collected the tithes. The mercenaries had already left a trail of destruction on their way there. They set fire to entire hamlets, drove out the residents and forced themselves on the women. Afra von Velseck, the Bishop's candidate for the abbess' office described the atrocities at length.[265] Afra's neutrality about this towards Verena von Stuben can be completely challenged.

In any case, the mercenaries left Enneberg and headed toward the monastery. On the way there, von Hornstein wanted to pillage more hamlets. In order get to the monastery they had to pass through a steep escarpment shortly after the Gasthof Oberpalfrad (an inn) and cross a gorge that was only spanned by a small wooden bridge.

What actually happened then is contentious in the research. The first summary description of the battle came from Mathias Burglechner from his history of Tirol written around 1620. There we learn something completely different. Ostensibly no mercenaries went back to the Sonnenburg Monastery, rather it was peasants from Enneberg who went there wanting to deliver their taxes. On the way there, they were attacked by Gabriel Prack, the Bishop's magistrate at Buchenstein (*Amtmann zu Buchenstein*). Although the peasants pleaded for mercy, Prack mercilessly killed every one of them.

This version of the story was later accepted by historians in later times without criticism, at most with the details modified.

Jobst von Hornstein's mercenaries then went on the trail to Oberpalfrad through the mentioned gorge. The approximate 60 peasants from Enneberg, who had retreated from the town in the face of the overpowering enemy, chose this location for an ambush. When the mercenary unit wanted to pass through the escarpment the peasants unleashed a devastating avalanche. There was no escape for the numerically outnumbered mercenaries. About 50 of the 80-man mercenary unit were killed by the rocks and the pursuing Ennebergers. But the peasants did not risk laying hands on the knight Jobst von Hornstein and just took him and the wretched remainder of his unit captive. The corpses were plundered and certainly not buried but left where they lie.

In the meantime, the Bishop's magistrate, Garriel Prack zu Asch had arrived with 200 mean as reinforcements, that in the other version had allegedly murdered the peasants. Using his men, Prack captured the Sonnenburg Cloister and was able to drive out the contentious Abbess Verena on 8 April 1458.

But that was not the end of the chapter, since the cloister remained in the Bishops' possession until 26 May. The sovereign Sigismund, who so far had at least officially stayed out of the conflict, had his troops occupy the Sonnenburg. On 15 June, Verena von Stuben was able to move back into the cloister as its superintendent.

Duke Sigismund and with him Abbess Verena von Stuben were victors in this conflict. Nicolaus Cusanus could not carry out his reform program against the will of the sovereign.

---

264 Ibid., p. 15.
265 Ibid., p. 21.

LIST OF THE PERSONS INVOLVED IN THE CONDUCT OF THE DUEL

On the Venetian side:

Antonio Maria da Sanseverino
Conte (Count) Gian Francesco da Tollentino, tournament warden and escort
Giovanni Francesco da Tollentino, overseer of tournament ground
Lucio Ciprito, overseer of tournament ground
Lucio Cornelio Malvezzi di Bologna, tournament warden
Julio Cornelio Malvezzi di Bologna, tournament warden and hostage
Ottaviano da Sanseverino (illegitimate son of Robert Sanseverino), hostage
Lucas Pisani (Venetian high official)
Petro Diedo (Venetian high official)
Francesco Diedo (Venetian high official)
Hieronimo Marcello (Venetian high official)
Andrea Marcello (former captain of Durazzo)
Conte Gian Francesco da Parni, overseer of tournament ground and escort
a servant of the just named as an escort
Tullio da Constantia, escort
Tullo (?), escort
Rütz von Tamp, escort
Pietro Quirini, escort
Lienelus, escort
Brabndelius, escort
Juliano da Codignola, weapons master, escort
Simon, Dolmetscher, escort
Anton von Bagäu, escort
Bilgrim Credenzer, escort
Ragon Marschalk, escort
Lucio Malipiero, escort
Julio Malipiero, overseer of tournament ground
Peter Salern, overseer of tournament ground and eight hired men, four trumpeters and four mule-drivers

On Tirol's side:

Johann von Waldburg-Sonnenberg, duelist
Burkhard von Knöringen, tournament warden (*Platzvogt*), overseer of tournament ground
Friedrich Kappler, tournament warden, overseer of tournament ground, escort
Walter von Stadion, tournament warden, overseer of tournament ground
Bero von Rechberg, hostage
Ludwig von Rechberg, escort
Veit von Rechberg, escort
Hieronymuns von Heimenhofen, hostage
Wolf von Asch, hostage
Johann von Königsegg, hostage
Count Ulrich von Montfort, escort
Count Johann von Saarwerden, escort
Count Jakob von Tengen, escort
Freiherr Ulrich von Sax-Hohensax, escort
Johann Truchseß von Waldburg der jüngere, escort
Hans von Pienzenau (Pienzenauer), escort
Friedrich zu Rhein, escort
Siegmund von Welsberg, overseer of tournament ground, escort
Johann Kaspar von Laubenberg, overseer of tournament ground, escort
Michael von Freiberg, escort
Georg von Freiberg, escort
Johann von Freiberg, escort
Wendel von Homburg, escort
Urs von Kudringen, escort
Wilhelm von Kudringen, escort
Diepolt Spät, escort
Caspar von Wallenfels, escort
Caspar Dorer, escort
Johann von Wellwart, escort
Wilhelm Auer, escort
Lutz von Habsburg (Habsberg?), escort
Simon von Vürdt (Pfirt?)[266], escort
Michael Russ von Russenstein, escort
Veit Moosreiner (Mosrainer), escort
Degenhardt von Offenstätten, escort
Johann Berthold von Reinach, escort
Leonhard Vetter, escort
Wilhelm Deutsch, weapons master, escort
Johann von Montfort's personal servant with four trumpeters and a drummer
(the information comes from the Chronicle of the Steward of Waldburg - *Chronik der Truchsessen von Waldburg*[267])

---

266 That was most probably Simon von Pfirt (Ferrette) from the Upper Alsace, born 1460, died 1521, per Walter, Theobald, *Die Grabschriften des Bezirkes Oberelsass von den ältesten Zeiten bis 1820*, (Gebweiler: Boltze, 1904), p. 140.

267 See Pappenheim, Matthäus von, *Chronik der Truchsessen von Waldburg* (Memmingen: Mayer, 1777).

BIBLIOGRAPHY

Anshelm, Valerius, *Berner Chronik*, Erster Band (1st Vol.) (Bern: L.A. Haller, 1825), p. 390.

Bächtiger, Franz, "Bemerkungen zum Widersacher des Eidgenossen von 1529", in: *Zeitschrift für schweizerische Archäologie und Kunstgeschichte*, Band 37 (Bern: J. E. Wolfensberger AG/Wolfsberg Verlag,1980), pp. 252–259.

Baum, Wilhelm, *Sigmund der Münzreiche, Zur Geschichte Tirols und der habsburgischen Länder im Spätmittelalter* (Bolzano: Athesia, 1987).

Bertolizio, Giorgio, *Dogi, Nullità al potere* (Rome: Lit Edizioni, 2013).

Bidermann, Hermann Ignaz, *Die Italiäner im Tirolischen Provinzial-Verbande* (Innsbruck: Wagner, 1874).

Boeheim, Wendelin, *Handbuch der Waffenkunde, Das Waffenwesen in seiner historischen Entwicklung von Beginn des Mittelalters bis zum Ende des 18. Jahrhunderts* (Leipzig: Seemann, 1890).

Brandis, Clemens Wenzeslaus, Graf zu, *Tirol unter Friedrich von Österreich* (Vienna: Franz Ludwig, 1821), pp. 15–16.).

Brandis, Jacob-Andrä, Freiherr von, *Die Geschichte der Landeshauptleute von Tirol* (Innsbruck: Wagner'sche Buchhandlung, 1850).

Brauer-Gramm, Hildburg, *Der Landvogt Peter von Hagenbach – Die burgundische Herrschaft am Oberrhein 1469–1474* (Göttingen: Musterschmidt, 2001).

Bundi, Martin, *Frühe Beziehungen zwischen Graubünden und Venedig (15./16. Jahrhundert)* (Chur: Gasser, 1988).

Carey, Brian Todd, *Warfare in the Medieval World* (Barnsley: Pen and Sword, 2006).

Clayton, Anthony, *Warfare in Woods and Forests* (Bloomington und Indianapolis: University Press, 2012).

Clauss, Martin, *Ritter und Raufbolde, Vom Krieg im Mittelalter* (Darmstadt: Primus, 2009).

Commynes, Philippe de, *Memoiren* (Stuttgart: Kröner, 1972).

Daublebsky von Sterneck, Moritz Ritter, *Geschichtlicher Anhang zur militärischen Beschreibung des Kriegsschauplatzes Tirol und Vorarlberg* (Vienna: Gerold, 1872).

Delbrück, Hans, *Geschichte der Kriegskunst im Rahmen der politischen Geschichte*, Band 4 (Berlin: George Stilke & Walter de Gruyter, 1920).

DeVries, Kelly, *Medieval Military Technology* (Peterborough: University of Toronto Press, 1992).

Dumler, Helmut, *Venedig und die Dogen* (Düsseldorf: Artemis & Winkler, 2001).

Egg, Erich, *Der Tiroler Geschützguß 1400–1600 (Tiroler Wirtschaftsstudien 9)*, (Innsbruck: Universitätsverlag Wagner, 1961).

Embleton, Gerry u. Howe, John, *Söldnerleben im Mittelalter*, Stuttgart: Motorbuch 1996. (Originally published as The Medieval Soldier : 15th Century Campaign Life Recreated in Colour Photographs (London: Windrow & Greene, 1994).

Fiedler, Siegfried, *Taktik und Strategie der Landsknechte, 1500–1650* (Augsburg: Bechtermünz, 2002).

Forcher, Michael, *Kleine Geschichte Tirols* (Innsbruck and Vienna: Haymon, 2012).

Fowler, Kenneth, *Medieval Mercenaries, Volume I* (Oxford: Blackwell, 2001).

Funcken, Fred and Liliane, *Rüstungen und Kriegsgerät im Mittelalter* (Munich: Prisma-Verlag, 1979).

Furrer, Norbert u.a. (eds.), *Gente ferocissima: Solddienst und Gesellschaft in der Schweiz (15.–19. Jahrhundert)* (Zurich: Chronos Verlag,1987).

Gismann, Robert, Die Beziehungen zwischen Tirol und Bayern im Ausgang des Mittelalters, Herzog Siegmund der Münzreiche und die Wittelsbacher in Landshut und München von 1439–1479 (Innsbruck: Universität Innsbruck, 1976).

Gober, Manuel, *Museo Storico Italiano della Guerra Rovereto* (Rovereto, 2008).

Gravett, Christopher and McBride, Angus, *German Medieval Armies 1300–1500* (Oxford: Osprey, 1985).

Gstraunthaler, Olt. Dr. Gerhard, *Die Schlacht bei Calliano am 10. August 1487, Zur Geschichte des Laudegg-Fähnleins von 1496*, at www.tiroler-schuetzen.at.

Guicciardini, Francesco, *The History of Italy* (Princeton: Princeton University Press, 1984).

Hallauer, Hermann,:*Die Schlacht im Enneberg, Neue Quellen zur moralischen Wertung des Nikolaus von Kues* (Trier: Kleine Schriften der. Cusanus-Gesellschaft 1969).

Hansjakob, Heinrich, *Der Waldshuter Krieg vom Jahre 1468* (Waldshut: H. Zimmermann, 1868).

Hay, Denys: *Europe in the Fourteenth and Fifteenth Centuries*, (London: Routledge, 1989).

Heath, Ian, *Armies of the Middle Ages, Volume 1*, (Worthing: Wargames Research Group, 1982).

Heath, Ian, *Armies of the Middle Ages, Volume 2 (The Ottoman Empire, Eastern Europe and the Near East, 1300–1500)* (Worthing: Wargames Research Group, 1984).

Hefner, Otto Titan von, *Geschichte der Regierung Albrecht IV., Herzogs in Bayern* (Munich: Wolf'sche Buchdruckerei, 1852).

Hegi, Friedrich, *Die geächteten Räte des Erzherzogs Sigmund von Österreich und ihre Beziehungen zur Schweiz, 1487 - 1499: Beiträge zur Geschichte der Lostrennung der Schweiz vom Deutschen Reiche* (Innsbruck: Wagner´sche Universitätsbuchhandlung, 1910).

Heller, Ferdinand (trans.), *Das glorreiche Unterfangen. Galeeren auf Bergfahrt zum Gardasee; Erzählung in zwanzig Bildern* (Trento: Curcu & Genovese , 2015).

Hewitt, John, *Ancient Armour and Weapons in Europe* (Oxford: J. Henry and J. Parker, 1860).

Hormayr, Joseph von, *Taschenbuch für vaterländische Geschichte*, Band 8 (Leipzig: Georg Franz, 1837).

Hürlimann, Louis, "Ulrich VII. von Hohensax (1463 - 1538), Gerichtsherr und Militärunternehmer" in *Thurgauer Beiträge zur Geschichte*, Band 135 (Frauenfeld: Historischer Verein des Kantons Thurgau, 1995), pp. 169–175.

Jäger, Albert, "Die Fehde der Brüder Vigilius und Bernhard Gradner gegen Herzog Sigmund von Tirol," in *Denkschriften der kaiserlichen Akademie der Wissenschaften*, Vienna: K.K. Hof- und Staatsdruckerei, 1859), pp. 233–301.

Jedelhauser, Philipp, *Beiträge zum Beginn und zum Ende der Herrschaft der Markgrafen von Burgau aus dem Hause Berg*, 2. überarbeitete Auflage (2nd revised edition) (Krumbach: Frick, 2017), pp. 4–5.

Koch, H.W., *Medieval Warfare* (London: Prentice-Hall, 1978).

Köfler, Werner, *Land, Landschaft, Landtag: Geschichte der Tiroler Landtage von den Anfängen bis zur Aufhebung der Landständischen Verfassung 1808* (Innsbruck: Universitätsverlag Wagner, 1985).

Knapton, Michael, *Venice and the Veneto during the Renaissance: the legacy of Benjamin Kohl* (Florence: Firenze University Press, 2014).

Kramer, Daniel Robert, *Das Söldnerwesen, Militärisches Unternehmertum in der Genese des internationalen Systems* (Wiesbaden: Springer Vorschau, 2010).

Kremer, Klaus, *Nikolaus von Kues (1401-1464), Einer der größten Deutschen des 15. Jahrhunderts* (Trier: Paulinus, 1999).

Kretschmayr, Heinrich, *Geschichte von Venedig*, 2. Band (Gotha: Perthes, 1920).

Krieg von Hochfelden, Georg Heinrich, *Geschichte der Militär-Architektur in Deutschland* (Stuttgart: Ebner & Seubert, 1859).

Krones, Franz von, "Johannes Hinderbach", in: *Allgemeine Deutsche Biographie*, herausgegeben von der Historischen Kommission bei der Bayerischen Akademie der Wissenschaften, Band 12 (1880), pp. 457–458.

Krones, Franz von, *Sigmund, Erzherzog von Oesterreich* in: *Allgemeine Deutsche Biographie*, herausgegeben von der Historischen Kommission bei der Bayerischen Akademie der Wissenschaften, Band 34 (1892), pp. 286–294.

Lachmann et al., *eyn rohr aus eisern stangen, Zur Geschichte des Stabringgeschützes „Faule Magd"* (Dresden: Verlag Zeit im Bild, no year).

Ladurner, P. Justinian, "Die Vögte von Matsch, später auch Grafen von Kirchberg" in: *Zeitschrift des Ferdinandeums für Tirol und Vorarlberg*, Ser. 3, Bd. 18 (Innsbruck: Tiroler Landesmuseum Ferdinandeum, 1873) pp. 5-159.

Ladurner, P. Justinian et al. (eds.), *Archiv für Geschichte und Alterthumskunde Tirols*, Band 2 (Innsbruck: Wagner´sche Universitätsbuchhandlung, 1850).

Lanzardo, Dario (ed.), *Ritter-Rüstungen, Der Eiserne Gast, Ein mittelalterliches Phänomen*, (Munich: Callwey, 1990).

Lichnowsky, Eduard Fürst von, *Geschichte des Hauses Habsburg, 8th Vol (8. Band - Kaiser Friedrich III. und sein Sohn Maximilian, 1477–1493)* (Vienna: Schaumburg und Compagnie, 1844).

Lühe, Hanns Eggert Willibald von der (ed.), *Militair-Conversations-Lexicon* (Leipzig: C. Brüggemann, 1833).

Mallett, Michael, *Mercenaries and their Masters* (London: Rowman and Littlefield, 1974).

Mallet, M.E. und Hale, J.R., *The Military Organisation of Renaissance State: Venice c.1400 to 1617*, (Cambridge and others: Cambridge University Press 1984).

Meier, Werner, "Eidgenössischer Solddienst" in Kroll, Stefan and Krüger, Kersten (eds.): *Militär und ländliche Gesellschaft in der frühen Neuzeit* (Hamburg: LIT, 2000).

Messner, Florian and Seehase, Hagen, *Die Ennetbirgischen Feldzüge* (Berlin: Zeughaus, 2018).

Messner, Florian; Ollesch, Detlef; Seehase, Hagen and Vaucher, Thomas, *Der Engadiner Krieg, Eine Reise in die Renaissance* (Eltville: RWM-Kompendium, 2016).

Meynert, Herrmann, *Geschichte des Kriegswesens und der Heeresverfassungen in Europa*, 3 volumes. (Vienna: Beck, 1868/69).

Miller, Douglas and Embleton, Gerry, *The Swiss at War, 1300–1500* (London: Osprey, 1979).

Miller, Douglas, *Die Landsknechte* (Bonn: Verlag Wehr & Wissen, 1980).

Mohr, Conradin von, *Geschichte von Currätien und der Republik „gemeiner drei Bünde"* (Chur: Verlag der Antiquariats-Buchhandlung, 1870).

Nell, Martin, *Die Landsknechte, Entstehung der ersten deutschen Infanterie* (Berlin: Eberling, 1914).

Nicolle, David, *Medieval Warfare Source Book: Warfare in Western Christendom* (London: Arms & Armour, 1999).

Nicolle, David and Rothero, Christopher, *The Venetian Empire 1200–1670* (Oxford: Osprey, 2004).

Nicolle, David and Embleton G. A., *Italian Medieval Armies 1300–1500* (London: Osprey, 1983; Oxford: Osprey, 2006.

Niederstätter, Alois, *Das Jahrhundert der Mitte. An der Wende vom Mittelalter zur Neuzeit* (Vienna: Unterreuter, 1996).

Oakeshott, Ewart, *The Sword in the Age of Chivalry* (Woodbridge: Praeger, 1964).

Oakeshott, Ewart, *European Weapons and Armour: From the Renaissance to the Industrial Revolution* (Woodbridge: Boydell Press, 1980).

Obermair, Hannes: Schriftlichkeit und urkundliche Überlieferung der Stadt Bozen bis 1500; in: Bozen Süd–Bolzano Nord. Band 2, (Bozen: LIT, 2008).

Ortenburg, Georg, *Waffen der Landsknechte, 1500–1650* (Augsburg: Bechtermünz / Verlagsgruppe Weltbild, 2002).

Paoletti, Ciro, *A Military History of Italy* (Westport and London: Praeger Security International, 2008).

Paulus, Christof, *Machtfelder, Herzog Albrecht IV. von Bayern (1447/1465–1508) zwischen Dynastie, Territorium und Reich* (Böhlau: Böhlau, 2015).

Parker, Geoffrey, *Cambridge illustrated History of Warfare* (Cambridge: Cambridge University Press, 1995).

Perini Agostino, *I castelli del Tirolo*, Band 2 (Milan: Pirotta 1839).

Pfister, Johann Christian von, *Geschichte von Schwaben, Neu untersucht und dargestellt, 2. Buch, 2. Abteilung* (Stuttgart : Daniel Class, 1827).

Planché, James Robinson, *An Illustrated Dictionary of Historic Costume: From the First Century B.C. to C. 1760*, vol. 1 (London: Chatto and Windus, 1876).

Procacci, Giuliano, *Geschichte Italiens und der Italiener* (Munich: C.H. Beck, 1989).

Prokop Freiherr von Freyberg, Maximilian, *Pragmatische Geschichte der bayerischen Gesetzgebung und Staatsverwaltung seit den Zeiten Maximilian I.* (Leipzig: Friedrich Fleischer, 1839).

Reid, William, *Buch der Waffen, Von der Steinzeit bis zur Gegenwart* (Düsseldorf and Vienna: Econ, 1976).

Remy, Andreas, "Descriptions of Battles in Fifteenth Century Urban Chronicles", in Curry, Anne and Bell, Adrian R., *Journal of Medieval Military History*, Vol. IX (Woodbridge: Boydell and Brewer, 2011), pp. 118–131.

Richards, John and Embleton, Gerry, *Landsknecht Soldier 1486–1560* (Oxford: Osprey, 2007).

Riedmann, Josef, *Das Mittelalter, Geschichte des Landes Tirol* Band 1, (Innsbruck: Athesia, 1985).

Roeck, Bernd, "Die Schlacht von Calliano; Mythos und Wirklichkeit", in *Der Schlern* – Zeitschrift für Südtiroler Landeskunde (Bolzano: Athesia, 1988), 12/1988, pp. 433-444.

Rudolph, J. Martin, *Die Hülfs- und Freischaarenzüge der Schweizer seit der Gründung der Eidgenossenschaft bis zum Einfall in den Kanton Luzern im Mai 1845* (Zurich: Leuthy, 1846).

Rudolph, J. Martin, *Kriegsgeschichte der Schweizer seit Gründung des Schweizerbundes bis zum ewigen Frieden mit Frankreich* (Baden: Zehnder´sche Buchhandlung, 1847).

Sandler, Stanley, *Ground warfare, An International Encyclopedia*, Vol. 1 (Santa Barbara etc.: ABC-CLIO, 2003).

Schaufelberger, Walter, *Der alte Schweizer und sein Krieg* (Zurich: Europa Verlag,1966).

Schlunk, Andreas and Giersch, Robert, *Die Ritter; Geschichte – Kultur – Alltagsleben* (Stuttgart: Thiess, 2009).

Schmid, Otto, *Pfarrkirche Wolfegg* (Regensburg: Schnell & Steiner, 1998).

Schmidtchen, Volker, *Bombarden, Befestigungen, Büchsenmeister* (Düsseldorf: Droste, 1977).

Schmidtchen, Volker, *Kriegswesen im späten Mittelalter, Technik, Taktik, Theorie* (Munich: VCH, 1995).

Schnitzer, Casimir, *Die Kirche des heiligen Vigilius und ihre Hirten; Kurze Geschichte des Bisthums und der Bischöfe von Trient* (Bozen: Eberle Joseph 1825), Band 1.

Seehase, Hagen and Ollesch, Detlef, *Kurfürst Friedrich der Siegreiche von der Pfalz (1425–1476)* (Petersberg: Imhof, 2013).

Seehase, Hagen und Ollesch, Detlef, *Die Burgunderkriege* (Berlin: Zeughaus, 2017); English Translation *The Burgundian Wars* (Berlin: Zeughaus, 2019).

Seehase, Hagen, "High Noon in Südtirol, Die Schlacht bei Calliano 1487", in: *Clausewitz*, Vol. 3/2017, pp. 40–44.

Shaw, Christine, *The Politics of Exile in Renaissance Italy* (Cambridge: Cambridge University Press, 2004).

Smith, Robert Douglas and DeVries, Kelly, *Medieval Weapons: An Illustrated History of Their Impact* (Santa Barbara and others: ABC-CLIO, 2007).

Speck, Dieter, *Kleine Geschichte Vorderösterreichs* (Karlsruhe: Lauinger Verlag, 2016).

Spreti, Vittorio, *Enciclopedia storico – nobiliare italiana: famiglie nobili e titolate viventi riconosciute dal R. Governo d'Italia, compresi: città, comunità, mense vescovili, abazie, parrocchie ed enti nobili e titolati riconosciuti* (Rome: Spreti, 1928–1936).

Strobel, Adam Walther, *Vaterländische Geschichte des Elsasses von der frühesten bis auf die gegenwärtige Zeit, Dritter Teil* (Strassburg: Verlag Schmidt und Grucker, 1843).

Strobel, Adam Walther, *Vaterländische Geschichte des Elsasses von der frühesten Zeit bis zur Revolution 1789* (Strasbourg: C.F. Schmidt, 1851).

Trapp, Oswald and Palme, Waltraut, "Burgbelagerungen in Tirol" in *Tiroler Burgenbuch*, Bd. 8 (Bolzano: Athesia, 1989).

Turnbull, Stephen, *The Art of Renaissance Warfare, From the Fall of Constantinople to the Thirty Years War* (Barnsley: Greenhill Books, 2006).

Urban, William, *Medieval Mercenaries, The Business of War* (London: Greenhill Books, 2006).

Vulpinus, Theodor, *Ritter Friedrich Kappler, Ein Elsässischer Feldhauptmann aus dem 15. Jahrhundert* (Strasbourg: J.H.E. Heitz, 1896).

Wagner, E., Drobna, Z. und Durdik, J., *Medieval Costume, Armour and Weapons* (London: Andrew Dakers, 1962).

Walter, Theobald, *Die Grabschriften des Bezirkes Oberelsass von den ältesten Zeiten bis 1820*, (Gebweiler: Boltze, 1904).

Weissinger, Rolf: *Die Schlacht bei Giengen, 19. Juli 1462, Die Geschichte eines vergessenen Krieges* (Stuttgart: KLIO Landesgruppe Baden-Württemberg, 1998).

Welber, Mariano, *La battaglia di Calliano 10 agosto 1487. Cronaca desunta dalle fonti narrative* (Calliano: Comune di Calliano, 1987).

Wiesflecker, Hermann, *Kaiser Maximilian I., Das Reich, Österreich und Europa an der Wende zur Neuzeit*, Band 1, (Munich etc.: Oldenbourg, 1971).

Wiesflecker, Hermann, "Die Grafschaft Görz und die Herrschaft Lienz, ihre Entwicklung und ihr Erbfall an Österreich (1500)," in *Veröffentlichungen des Tiroler Landesmuseums Ferdinandeum*, 78/1998, (Innsbruck: Tiroler Landesmuseums Ferdinandeum, 1998).

Wiesflecker, Hermann, *Österreich im Zeitalter Maximilians* (Munich: Oldenbourg, 1999).

Wilkinson, Frederick, *Alles über Handfeuerwaffen* (Zöllikon: Albatross Verlag, 1977).

Witte, Heinrich, "Zur Geschichte der Burgunderkriege", in *Zeitschrift für die Geschichte des Oberrheins* (Freiburg im Breisgau: Braun´sche Hofbuchhandlung, 1891), pp. 2–81.

Wolf, Susanne, *Die Doppelregierung Kaiser Friedrich III. und König Maximilian (1487–1493)* (Cologne, Weimar and Vienna: Böhlau, 2005).

Würdinger, Joseph, *Kriegsgeschichte von Bayern, Franken, Pfalz und Schwaben von 1347 bis 1506*, Band 2 (Munich: Cotta'sche Buchhandlung, 1868).